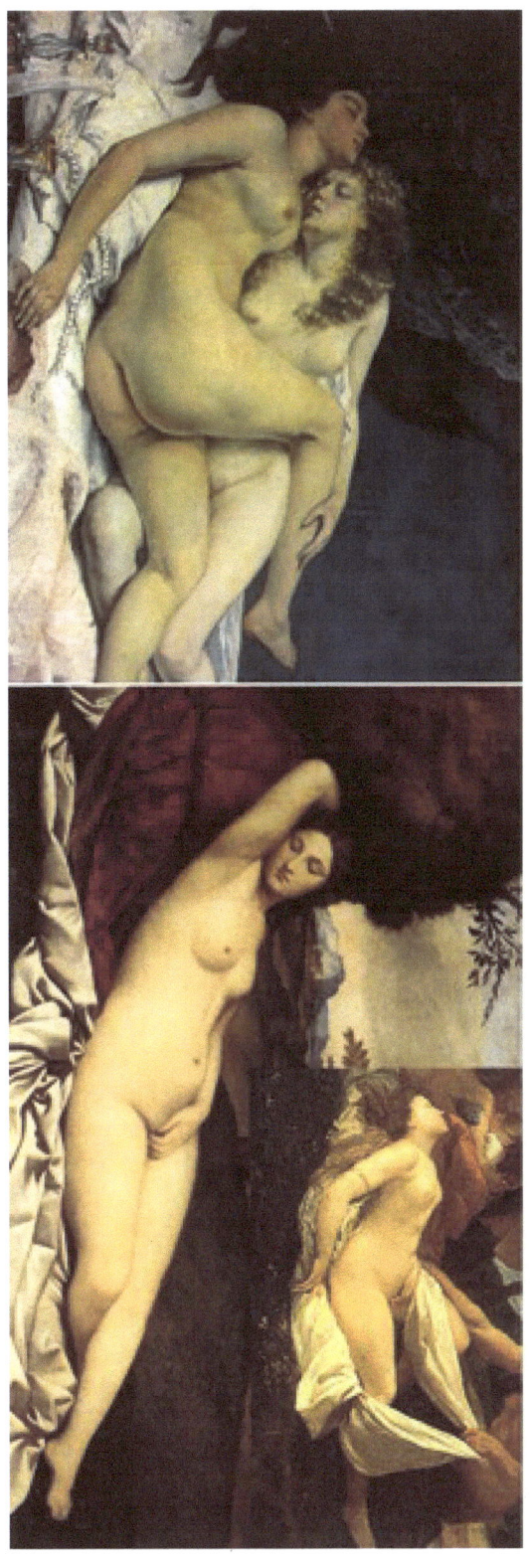

Sleepers in Art
Linda Savage

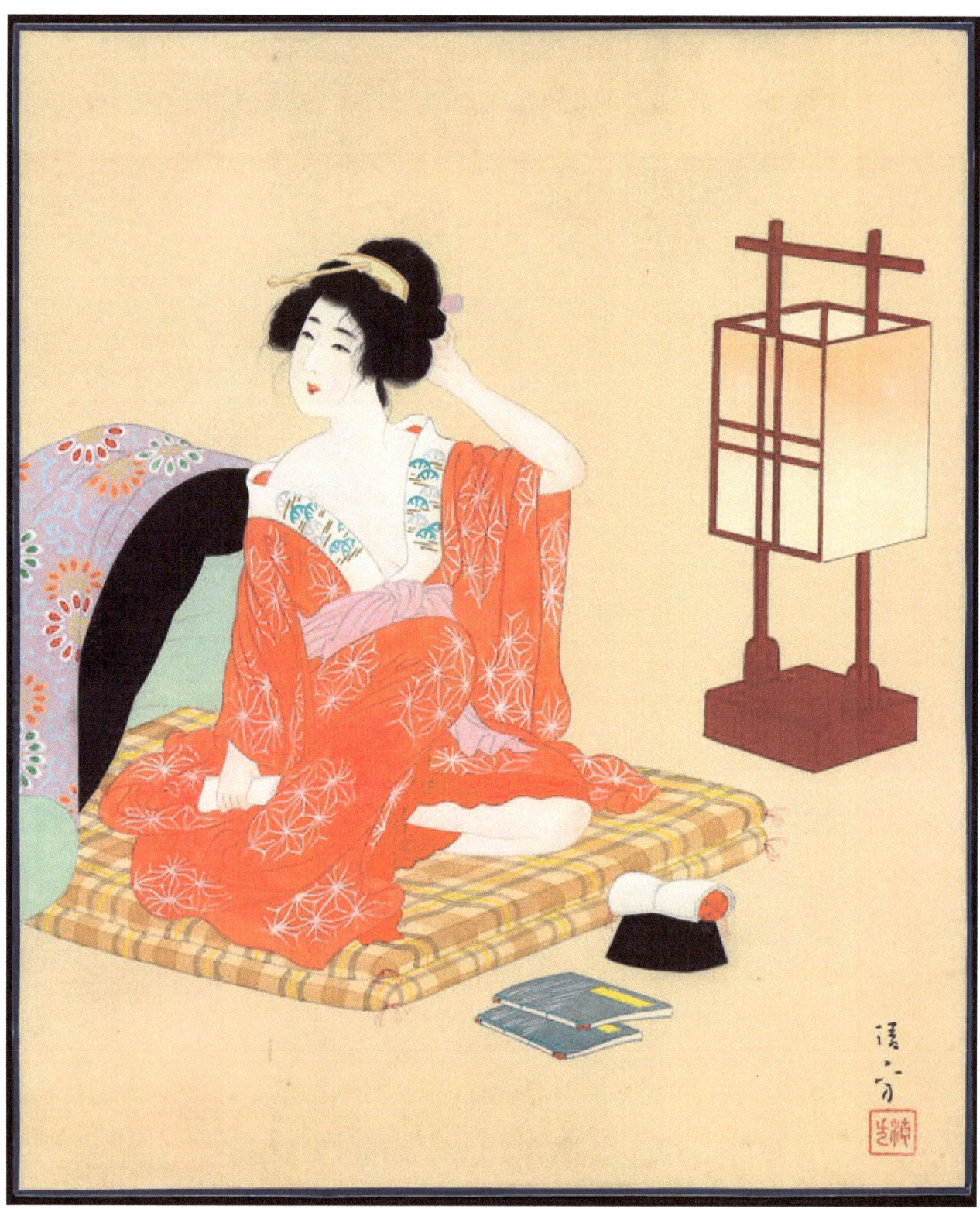

Bijin Preparing for Sleep--Kiyokata Kaburagi--Shin-hanga

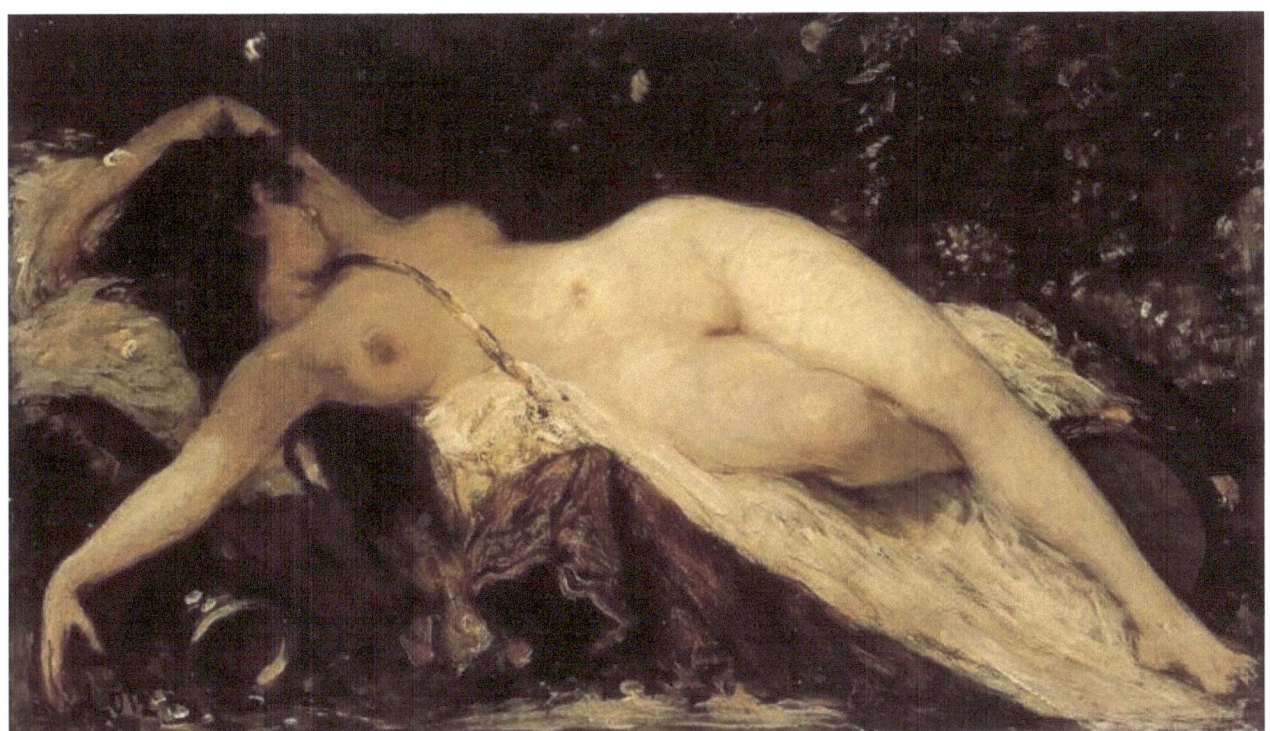

Sleeping Bacchant-- --Lotz Károly Antal Pál

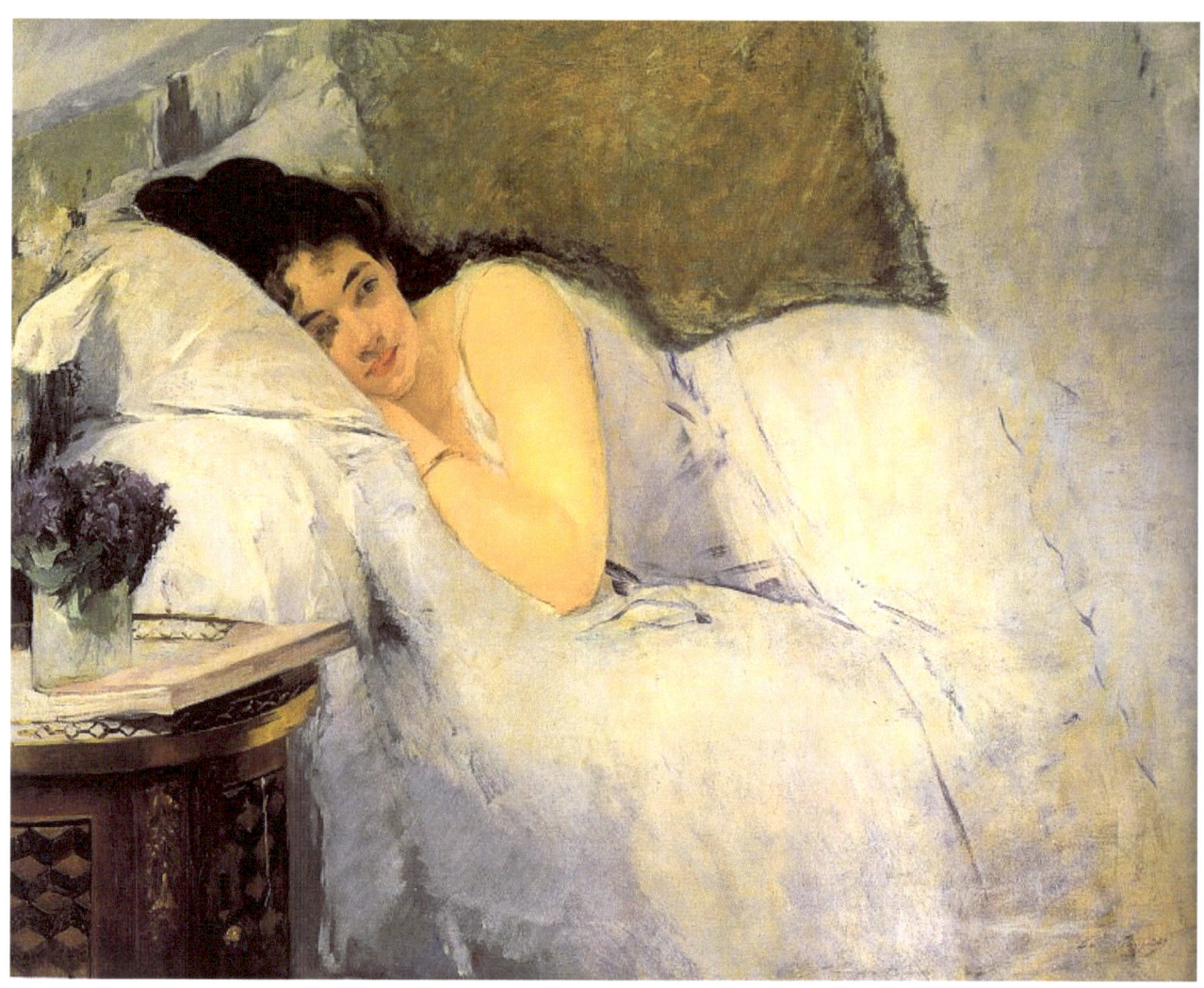

Woman Awakening--Eva Gonzales—1876--Impressionism

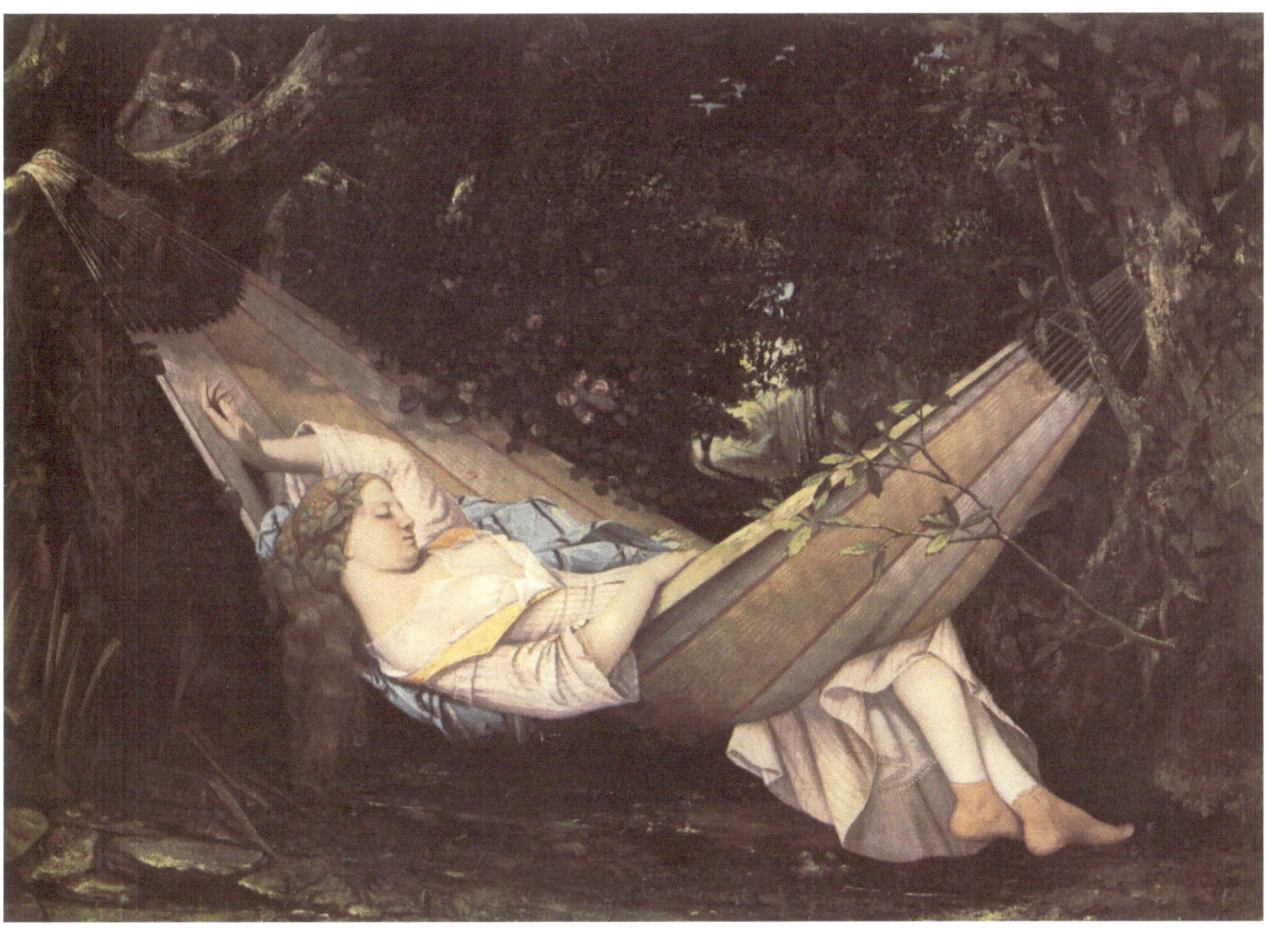

The Hammock--Gustave Courbet—1844--Romanticism

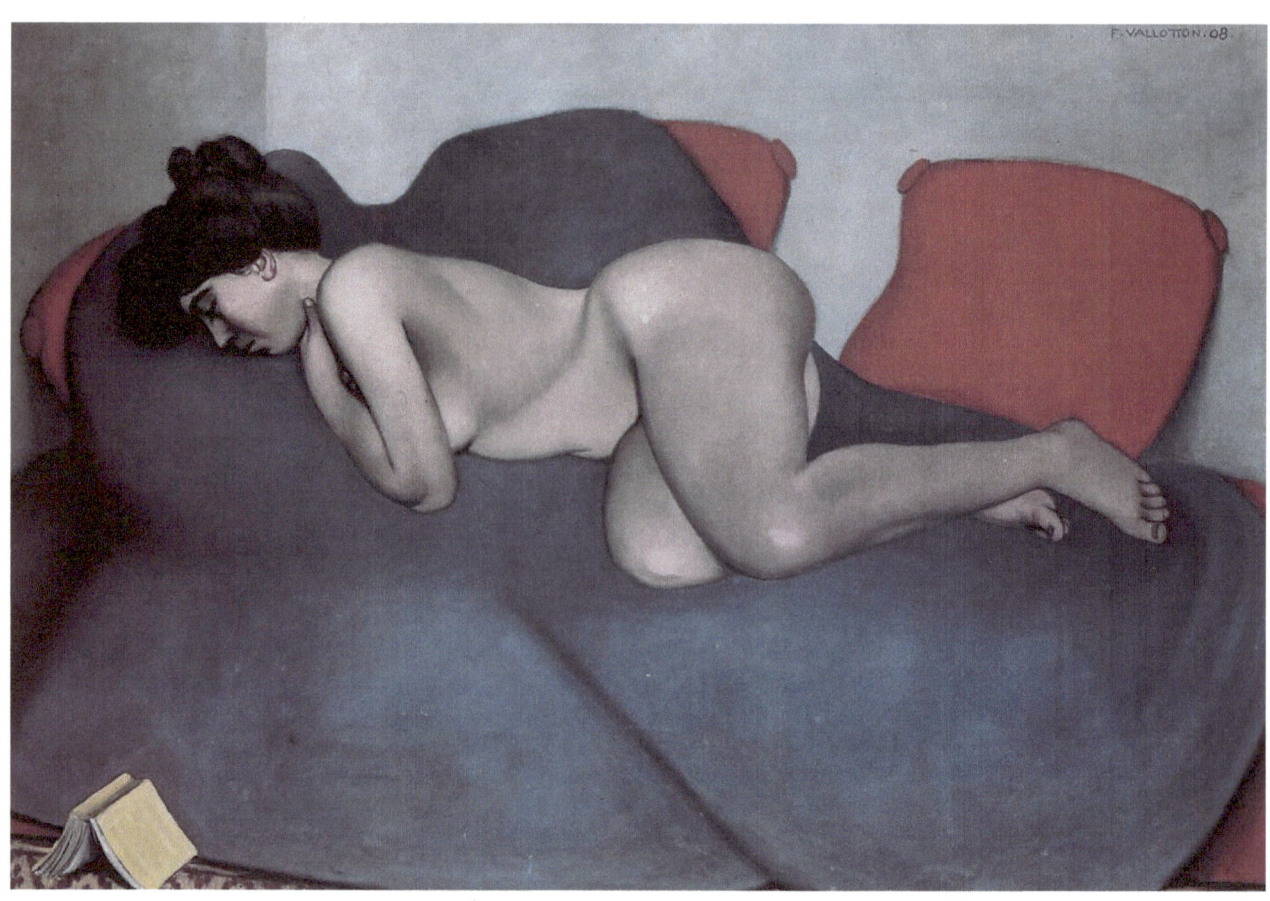

Sleep -Felix Vallotton—1908--Magic Realism

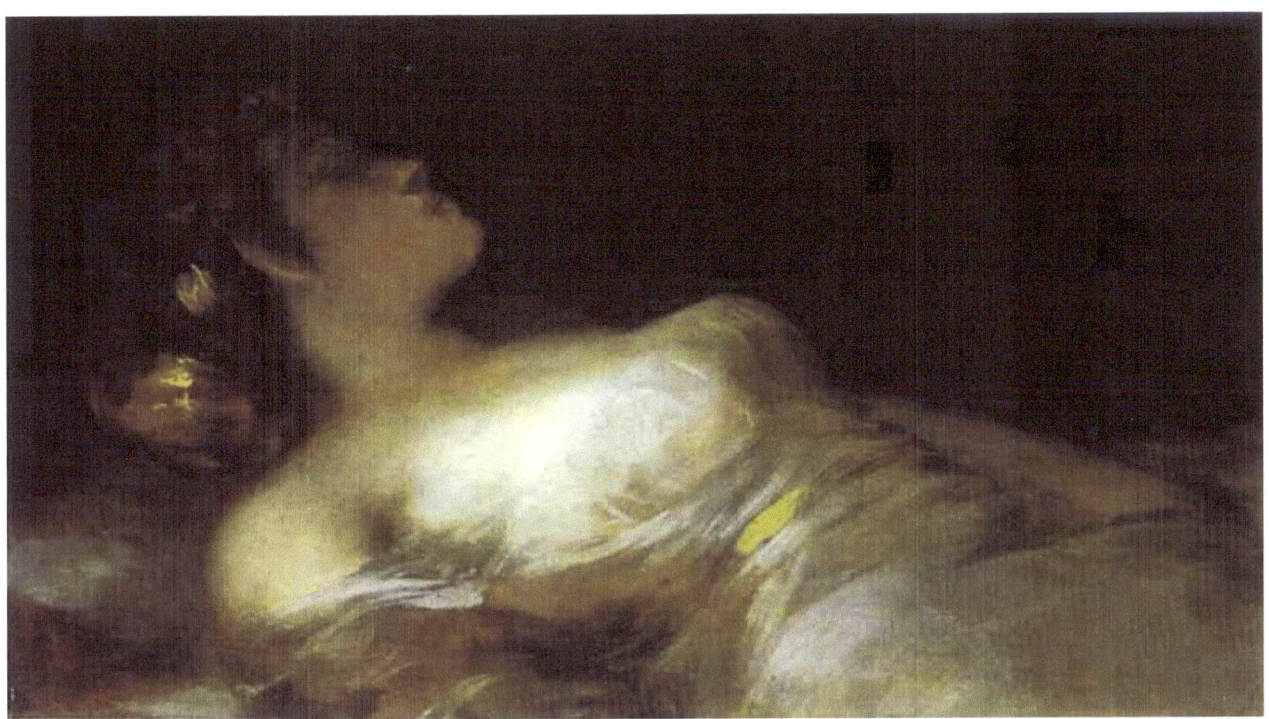

Sleep--Francisco Goya--Romanticism

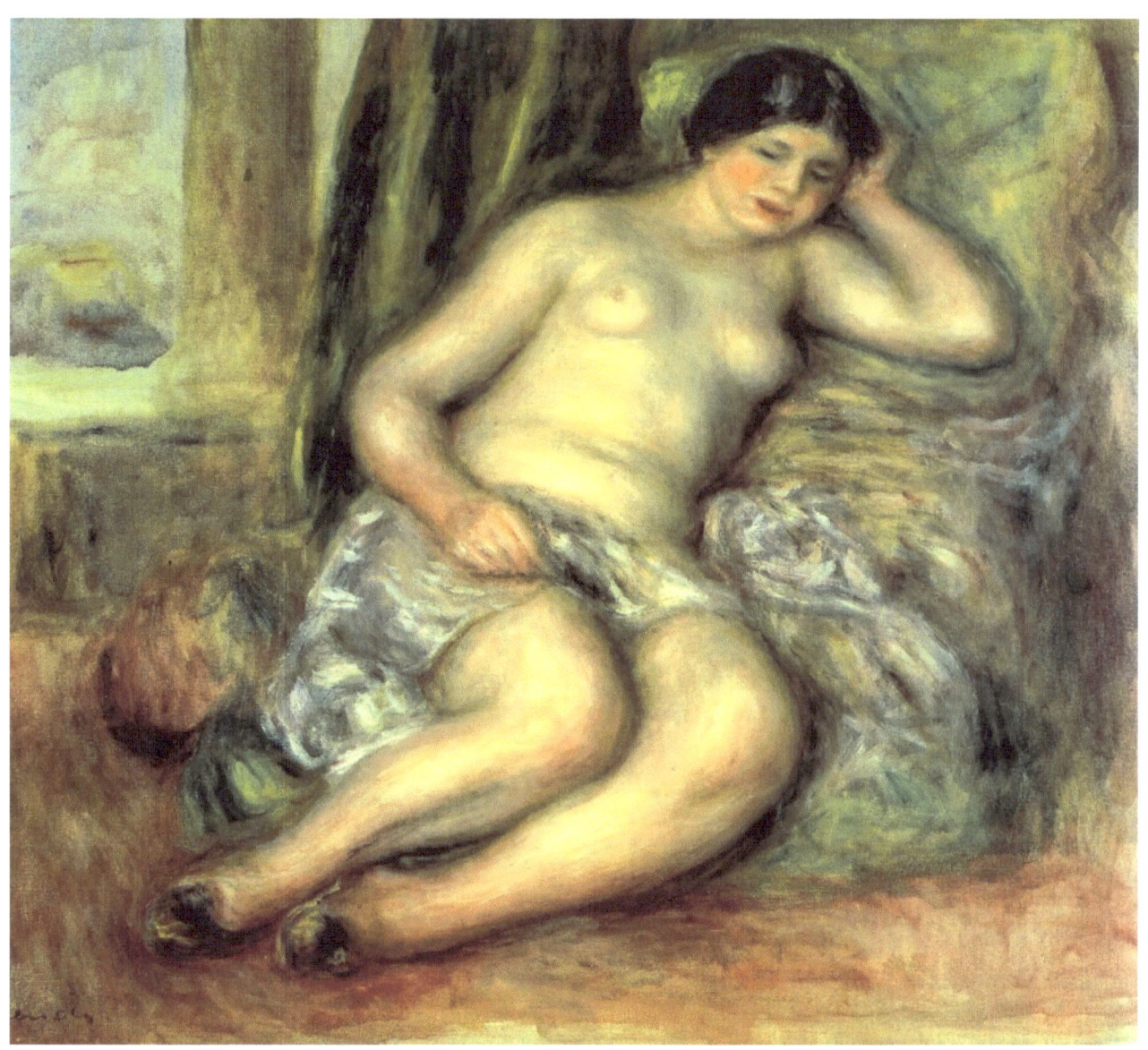

Sleeping Odalisque (Odalisque with Babouches)--Pierre-Auguste Renoir--1917

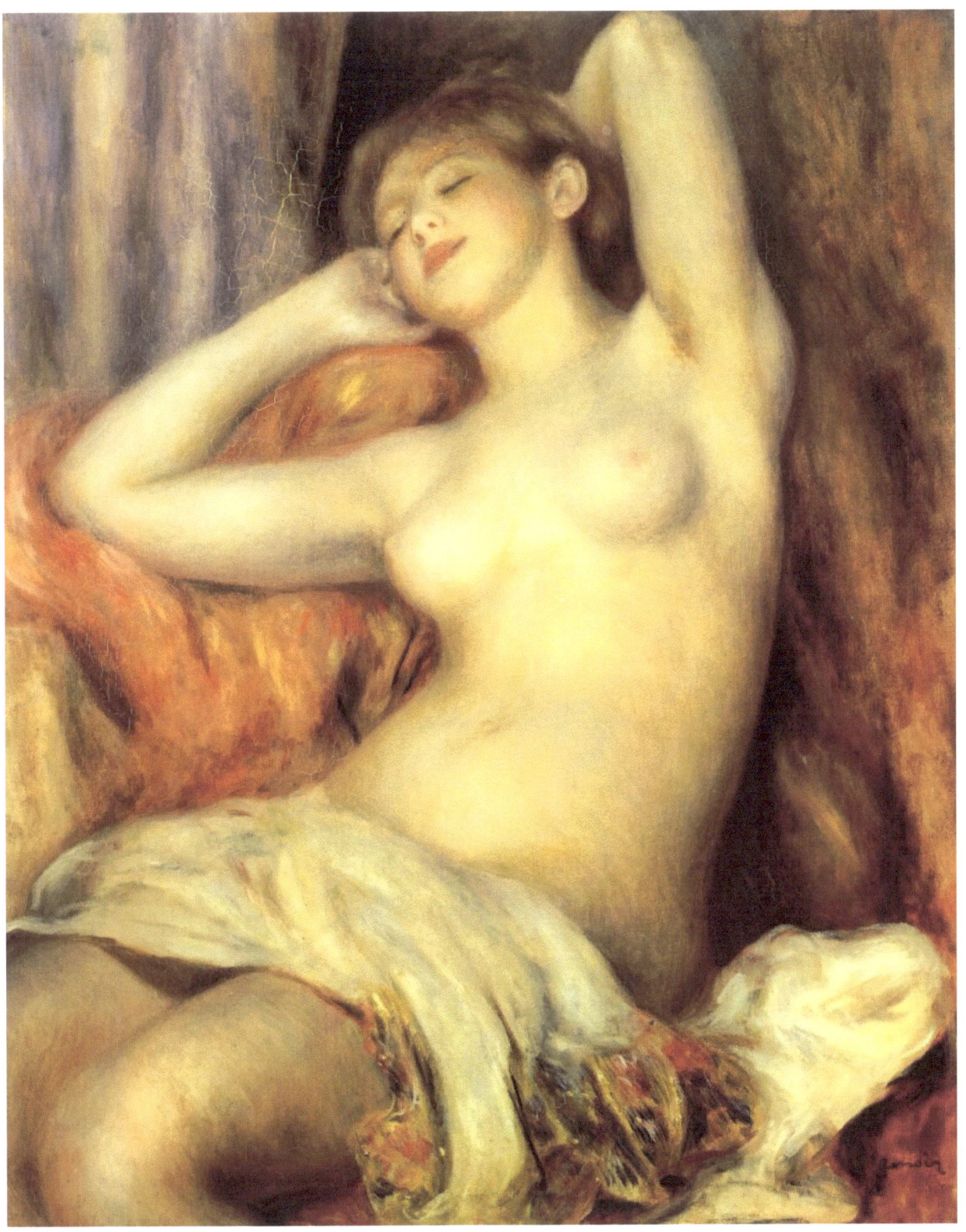

Sleeping woman--Pierre-Auguste Renoir—1897--Impressionism

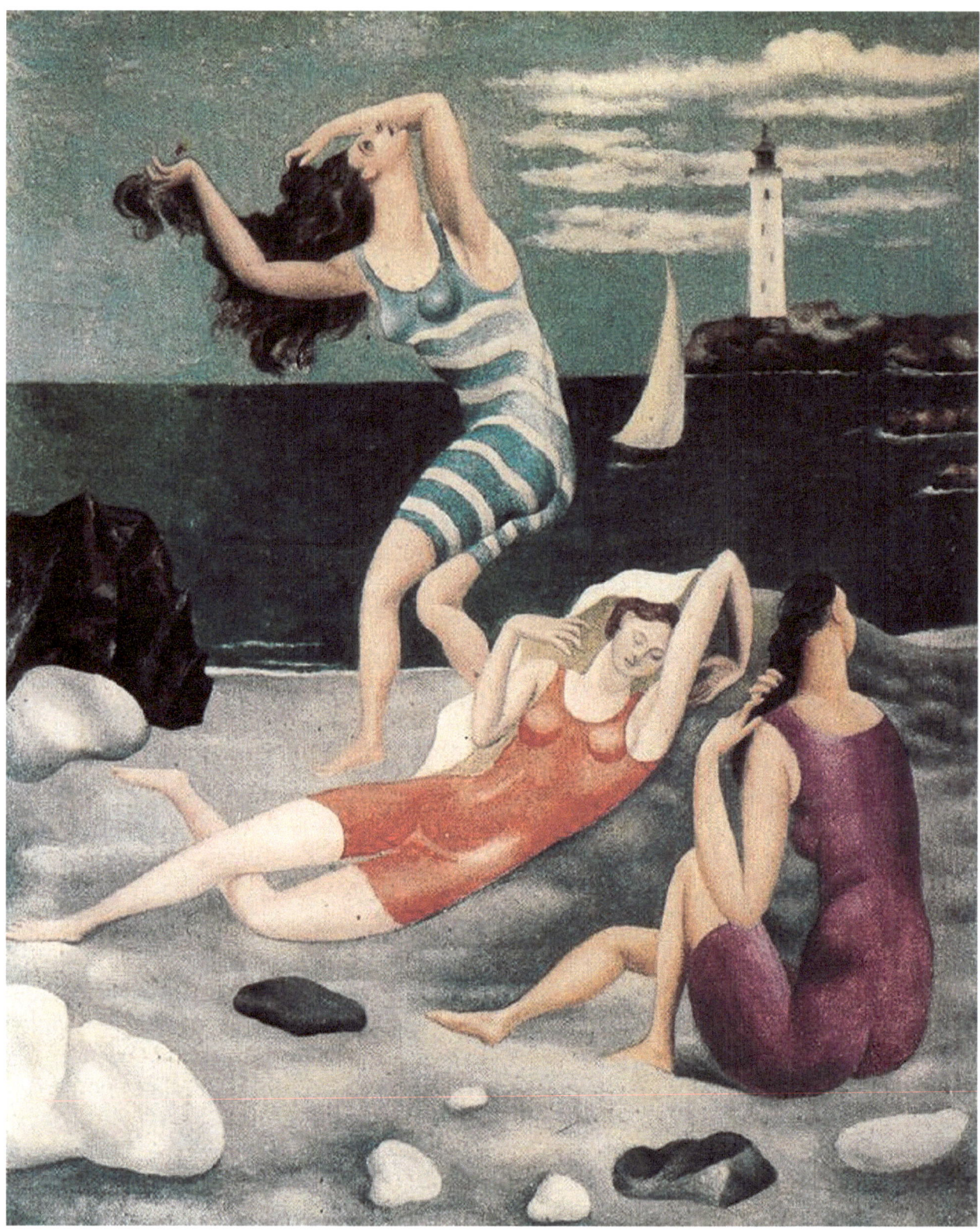

Bathers--Pablo Picasso—1918--Neoclassicism

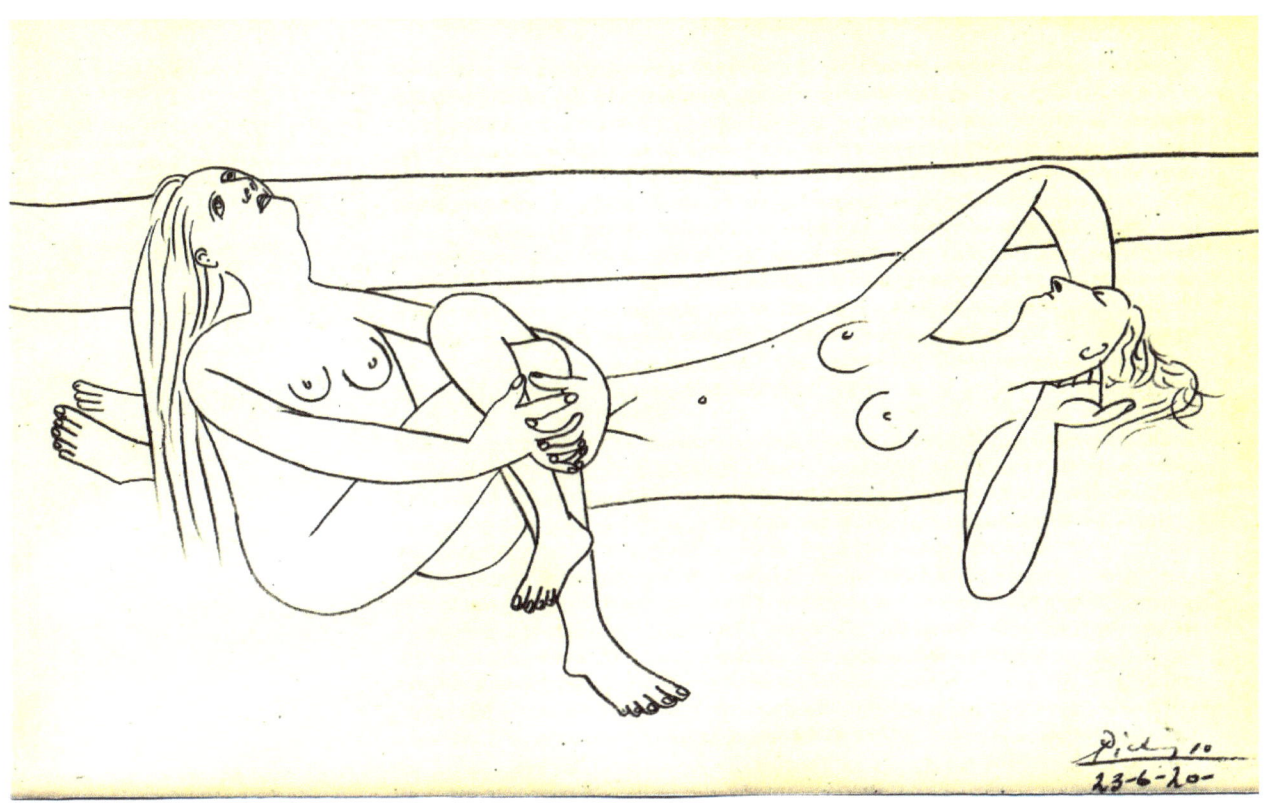

Nudes in Reverie--Pablo Picasso—1920--Naïve Art (Primitivism)

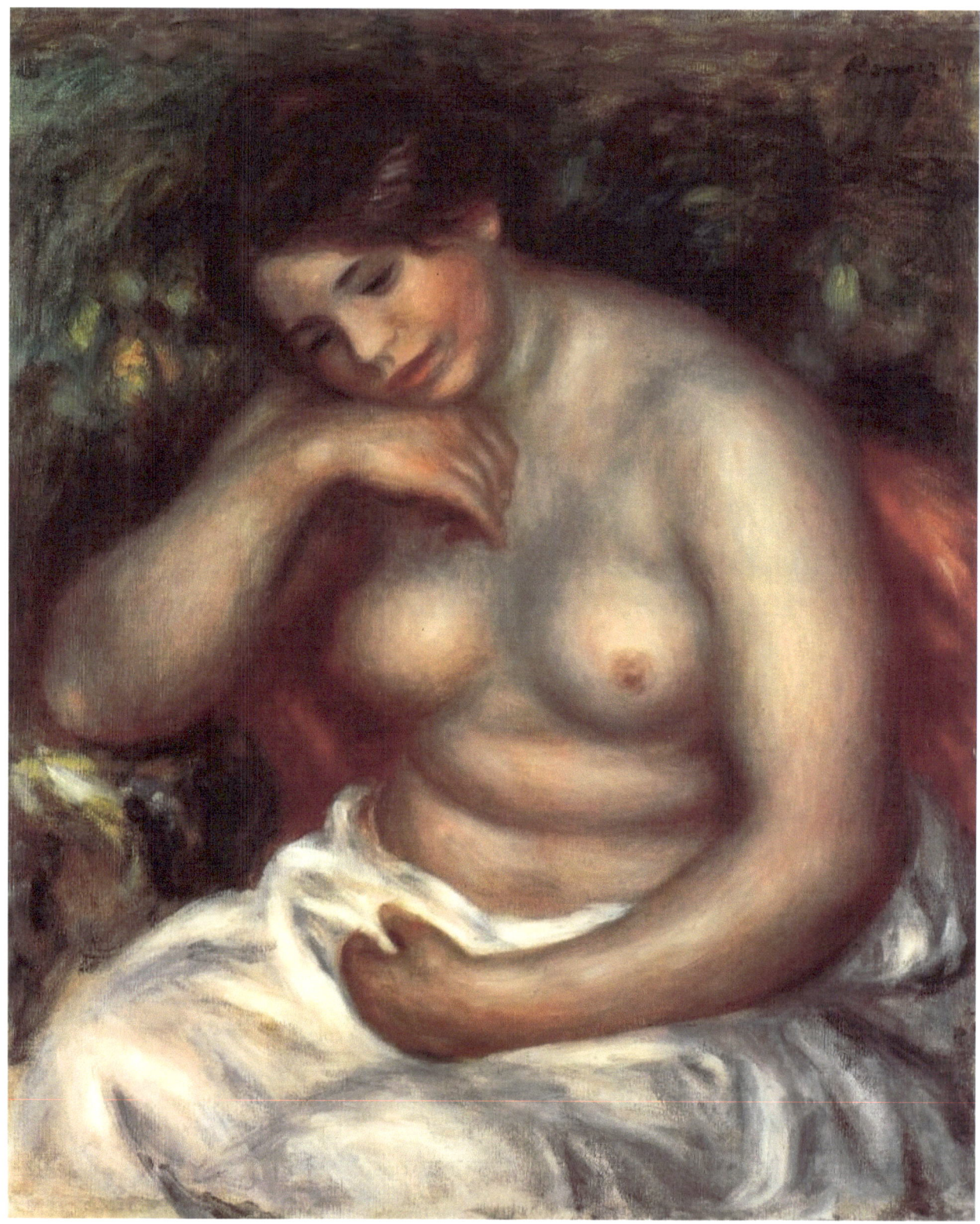

Woman sleeping--Pierre-Auguste Renoir—1900--Impressionism

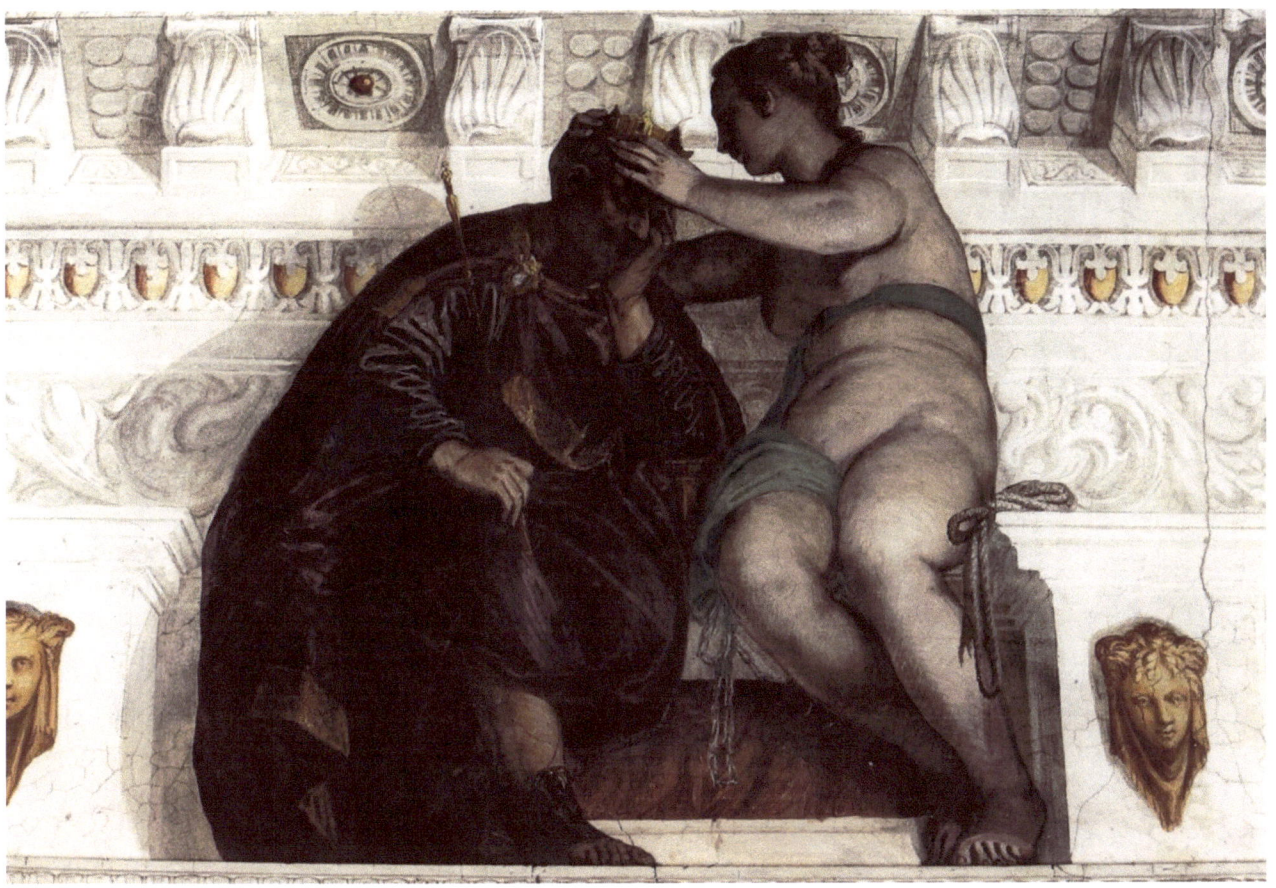

Chance Crowning a Sleeping Man--Paolo Veronese—1561--Mannerism (Late Renaissance)

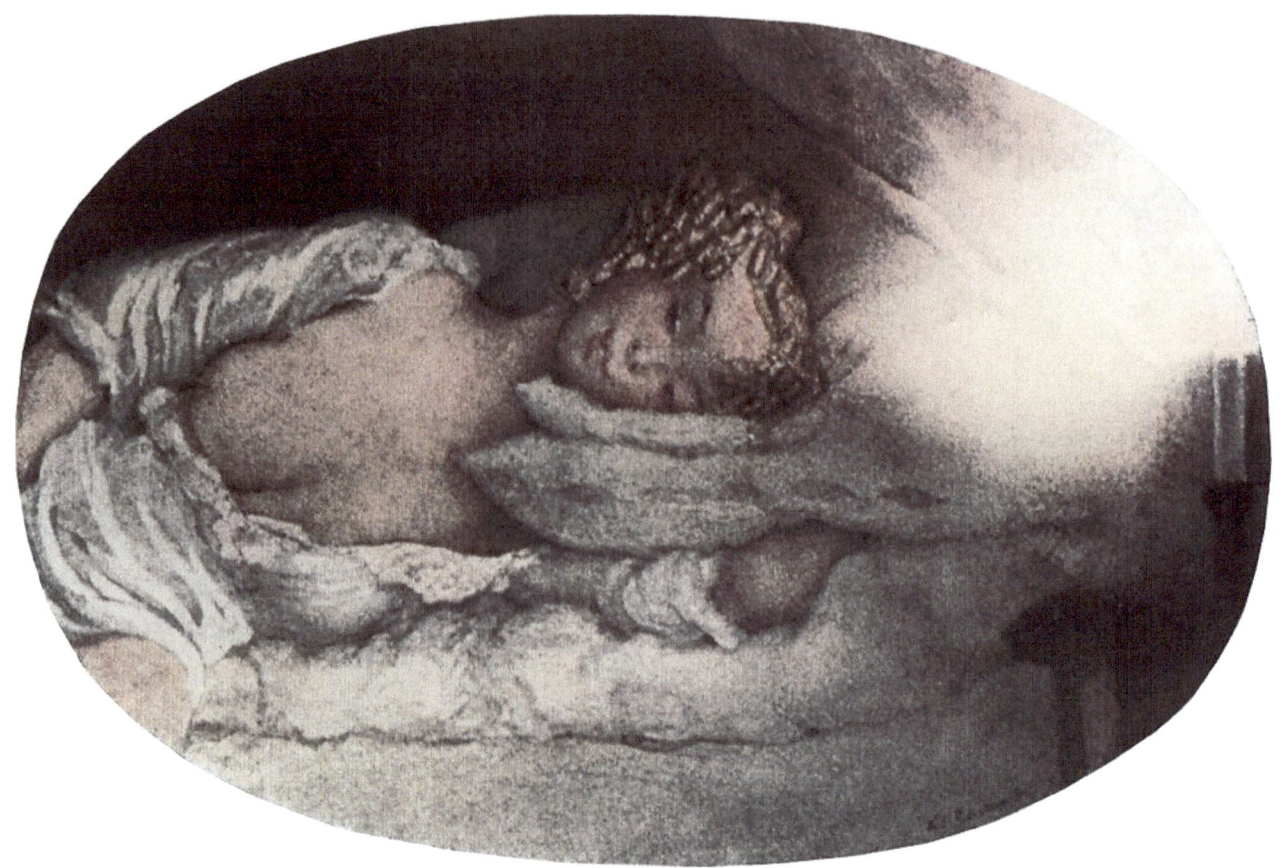

Natalia Pavlovna--Konstantin Somov—1899--Symbolism

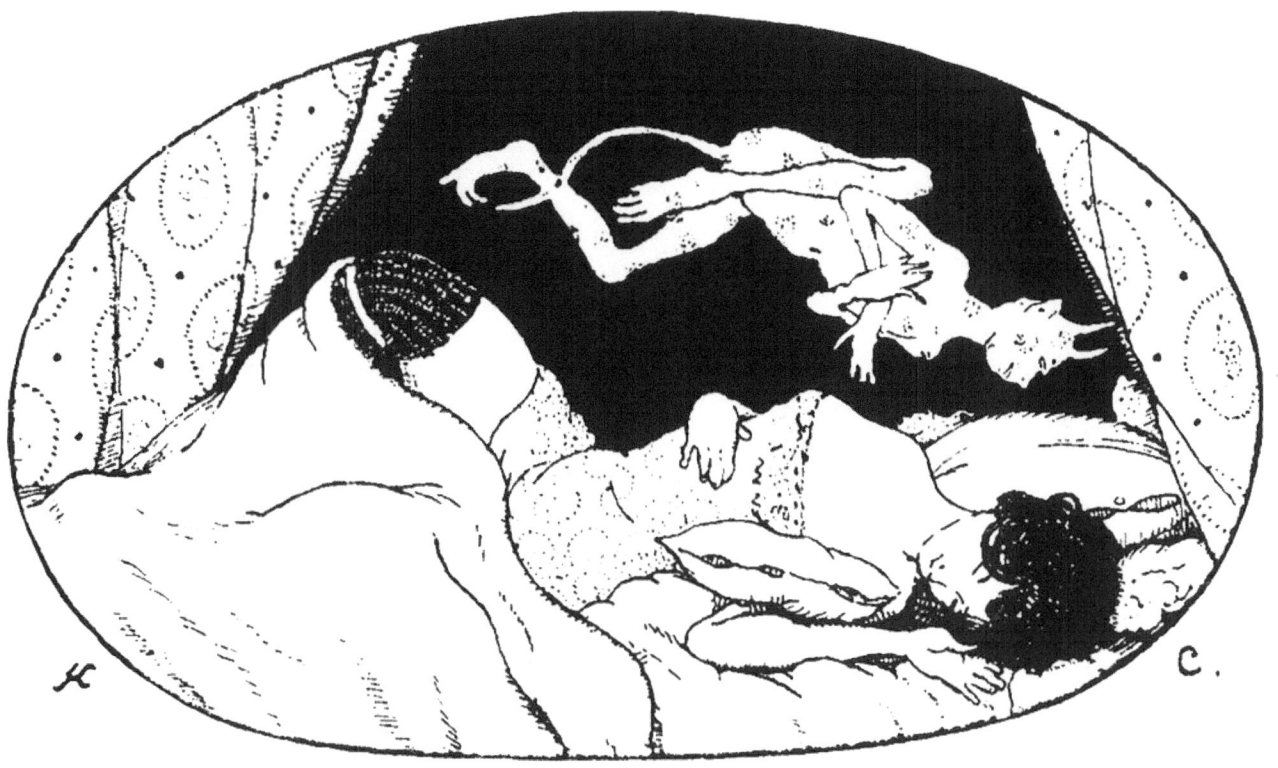

Sleeping Lady with the Devils--Konstantin Somov—1906--Symbolism

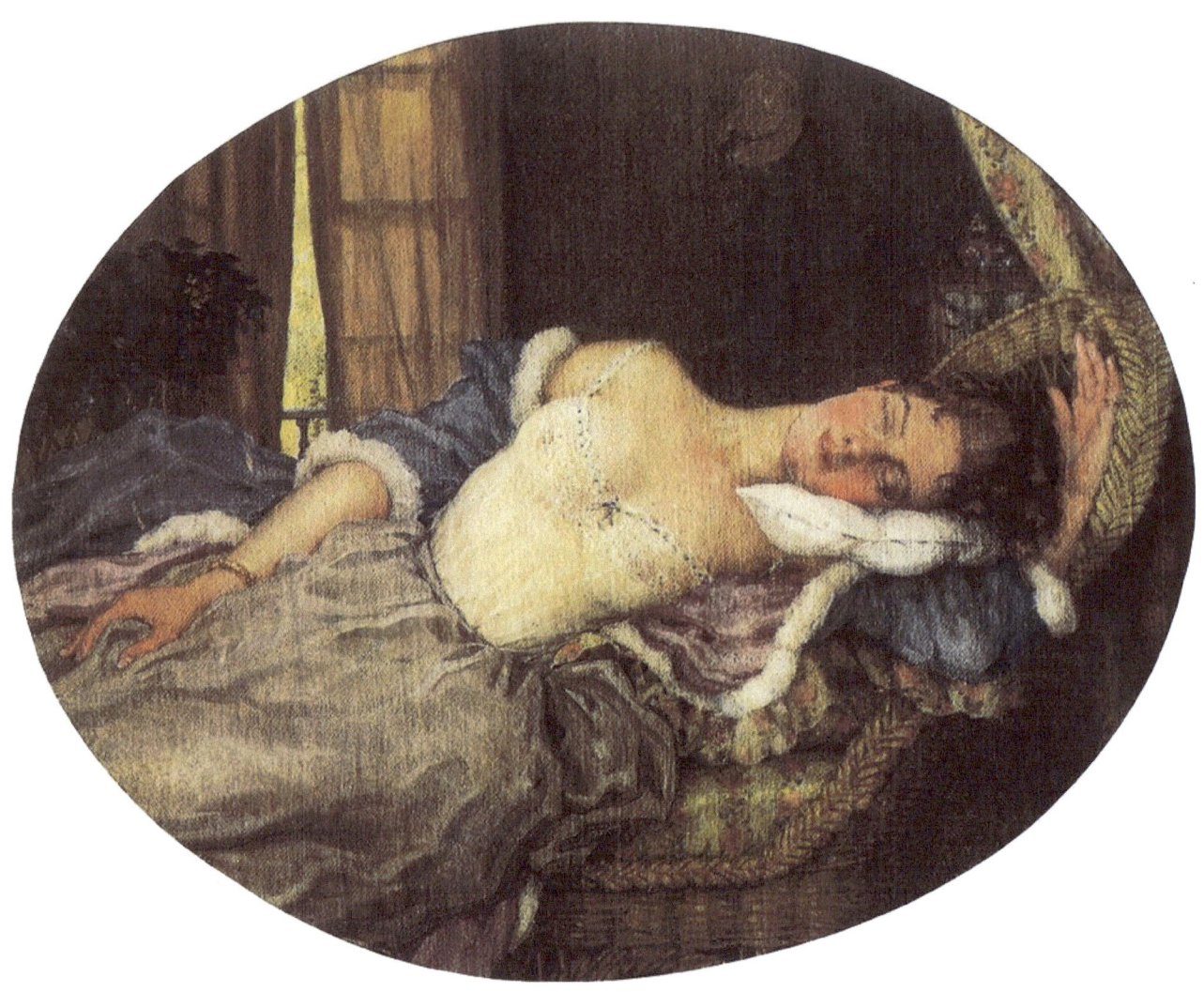

Sleeping Young Woman--Konstantin Somov—1922--Symbolism

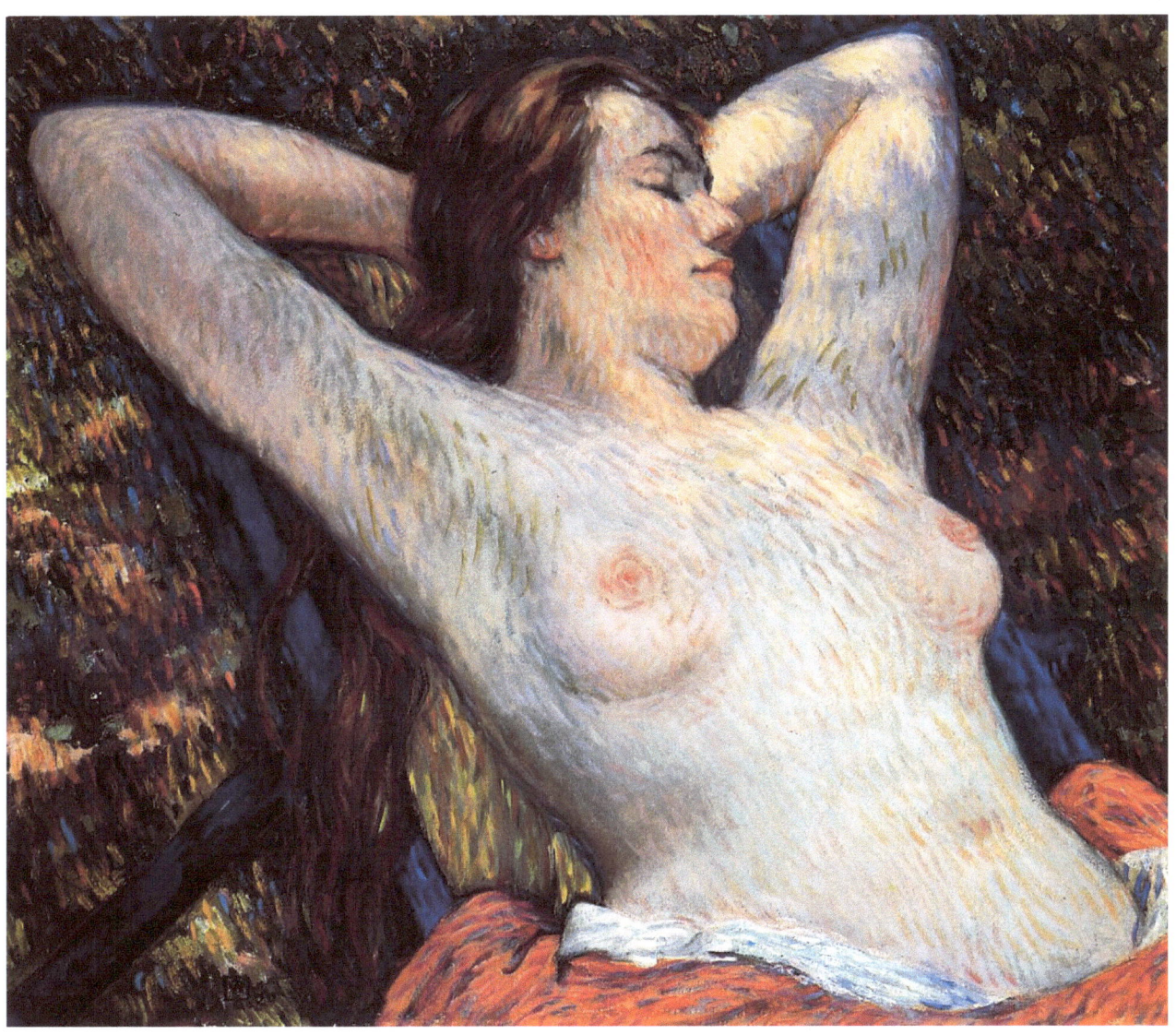

The Model's Siesta--Theo van Rysselberghe—1920--Post-Impressionism

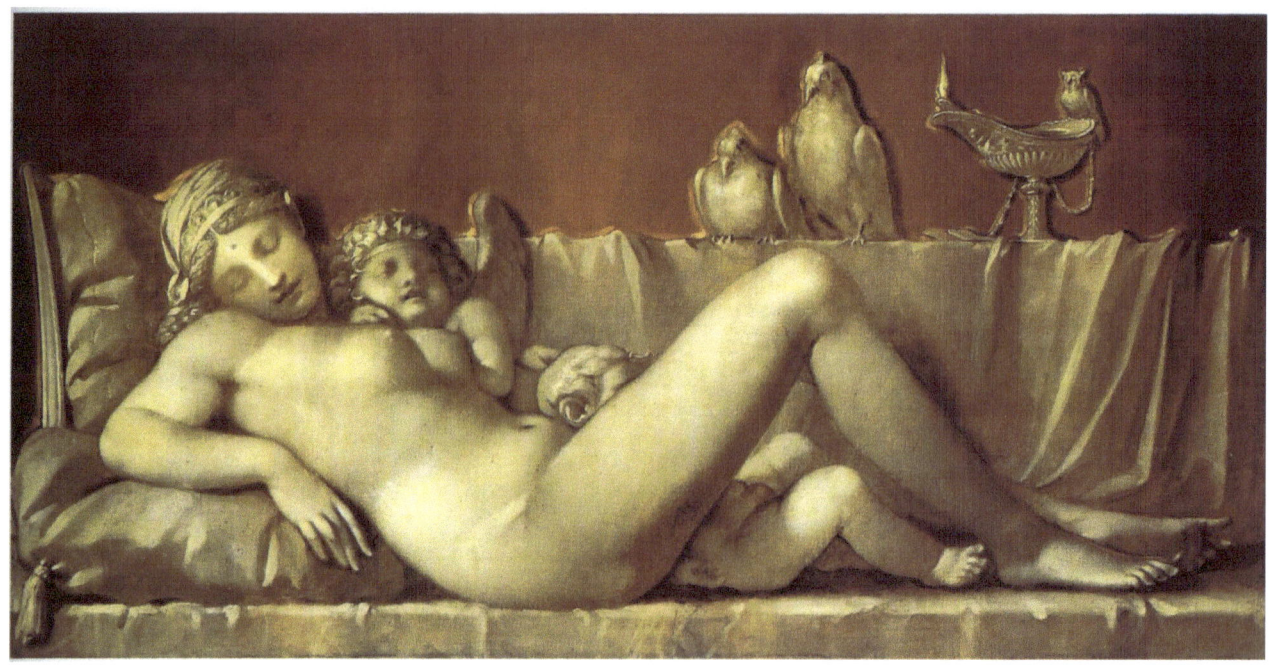

The Night--Pierre-Paul Prud'hon--Neoclassicism

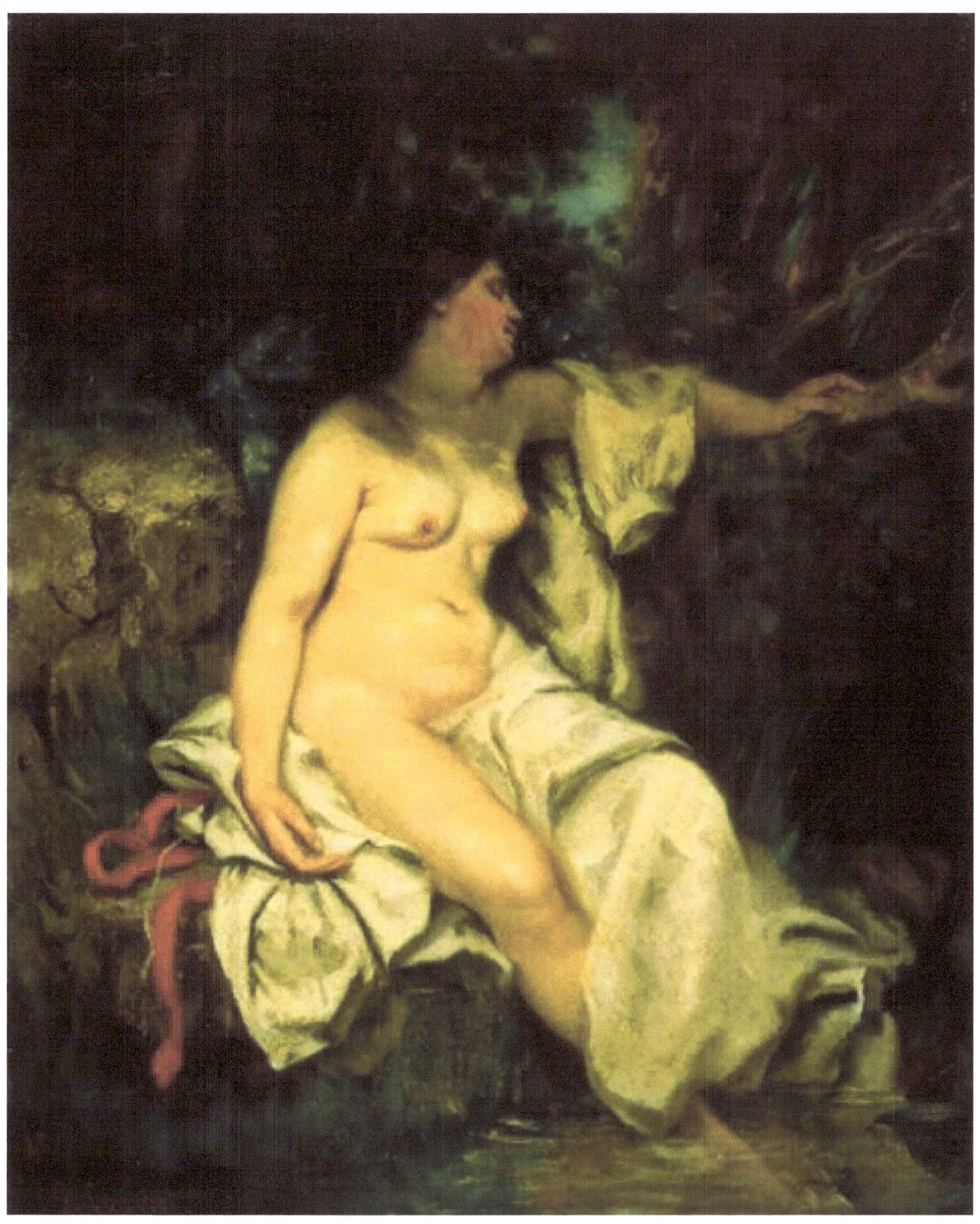

Bather Sleeping by a Brook --Gustave Courbet--Romanticism

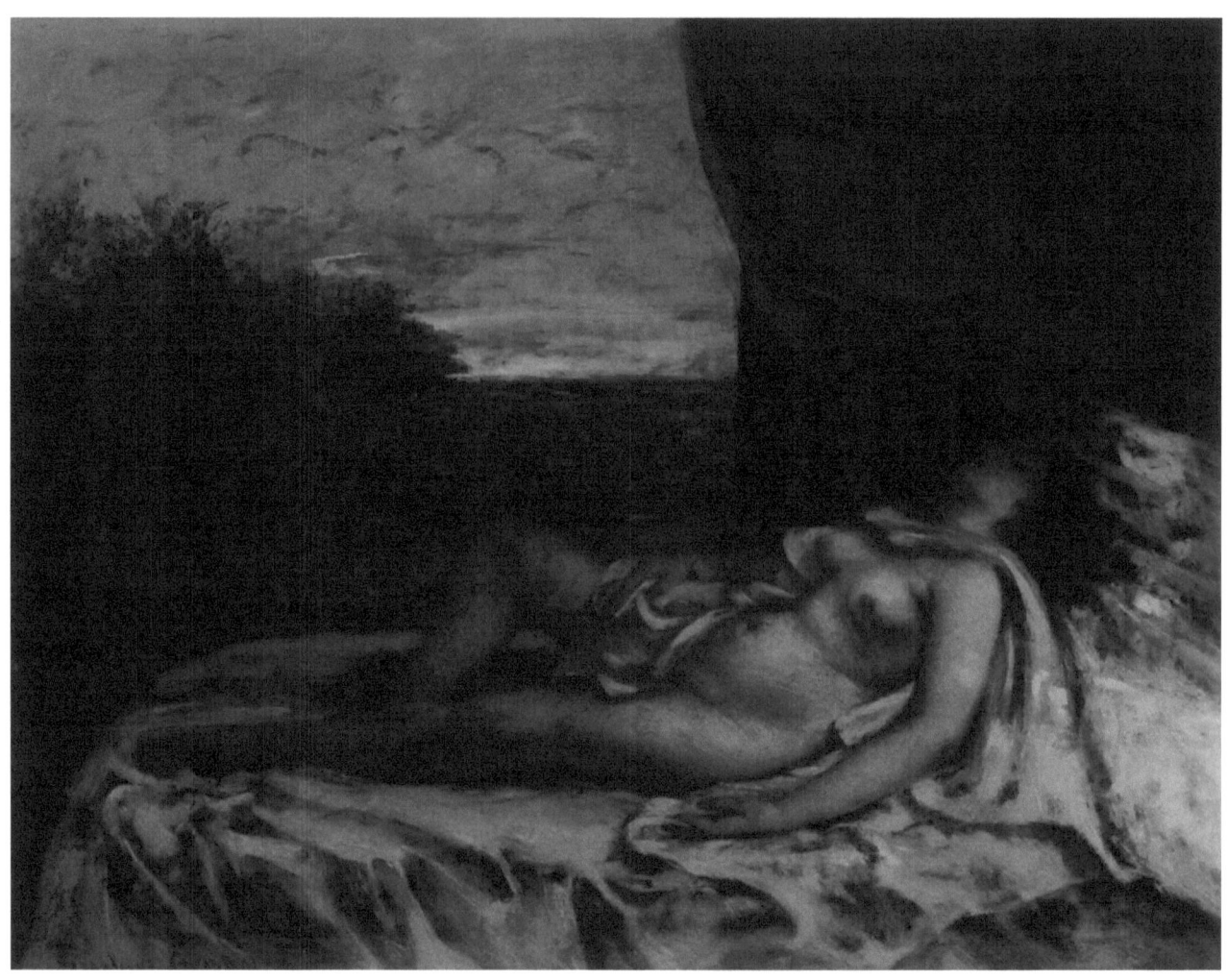

Sleeping Nude--Gustave Courbet--Realism

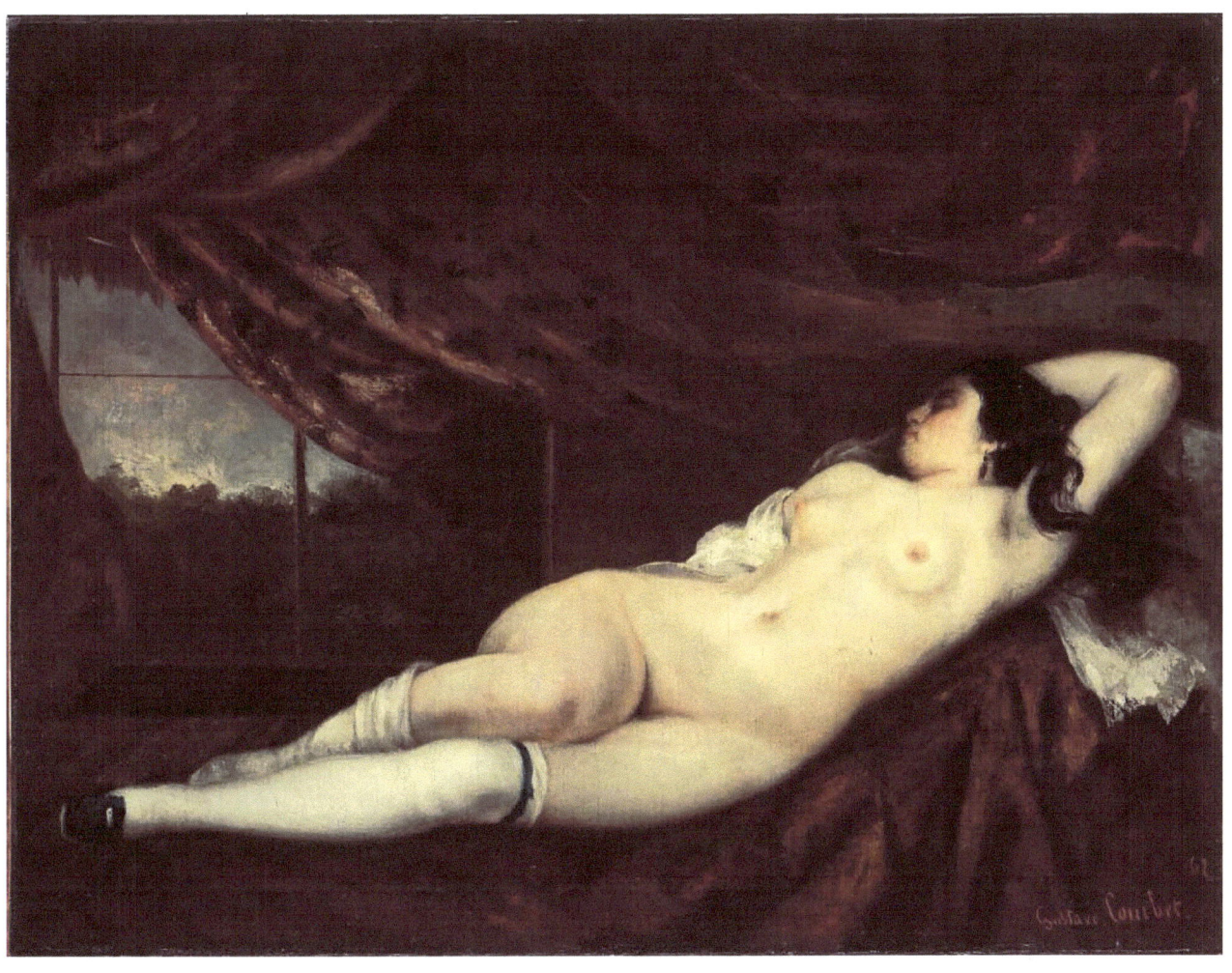

Sleeping Nude Woman--Gustave Courbet—1862--Realism

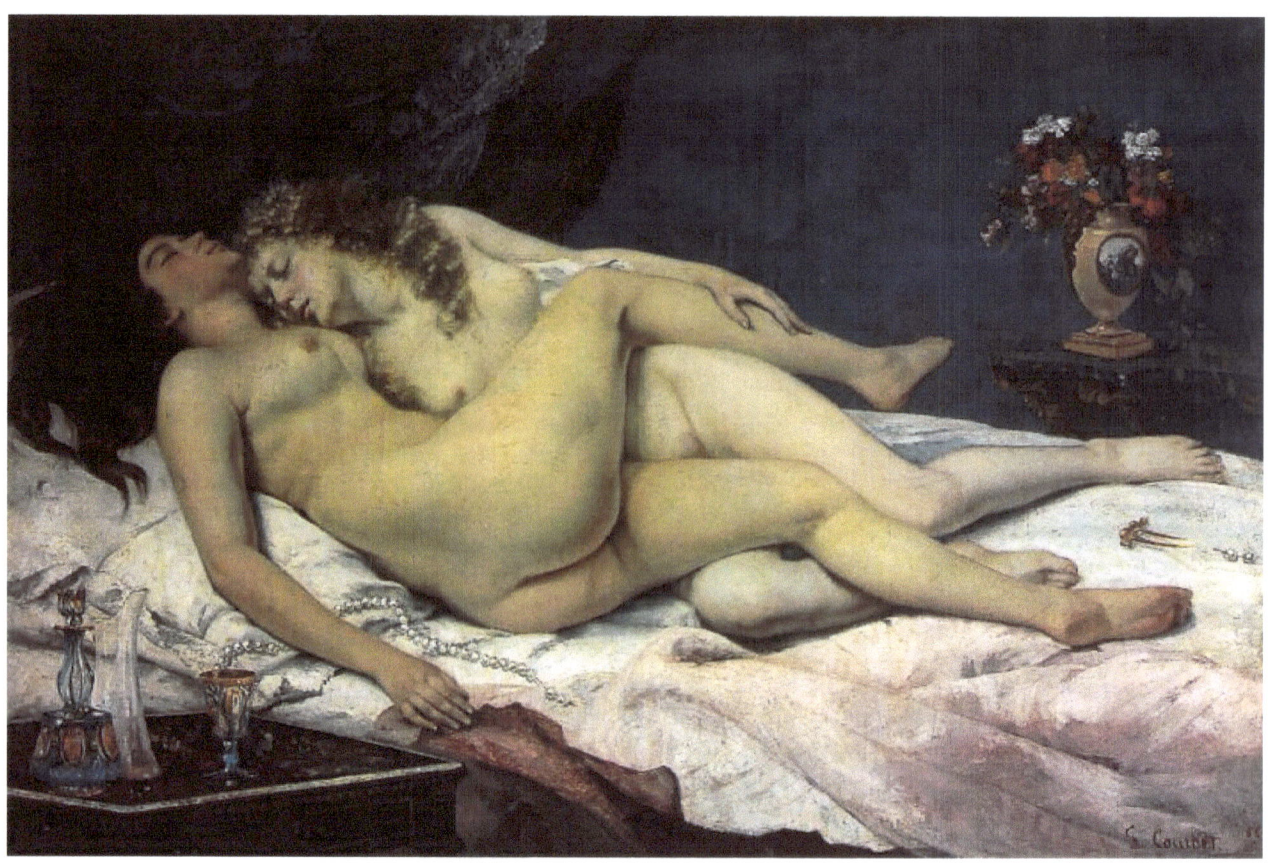

The Sleepers--Gustave Courbet—1866--Realism

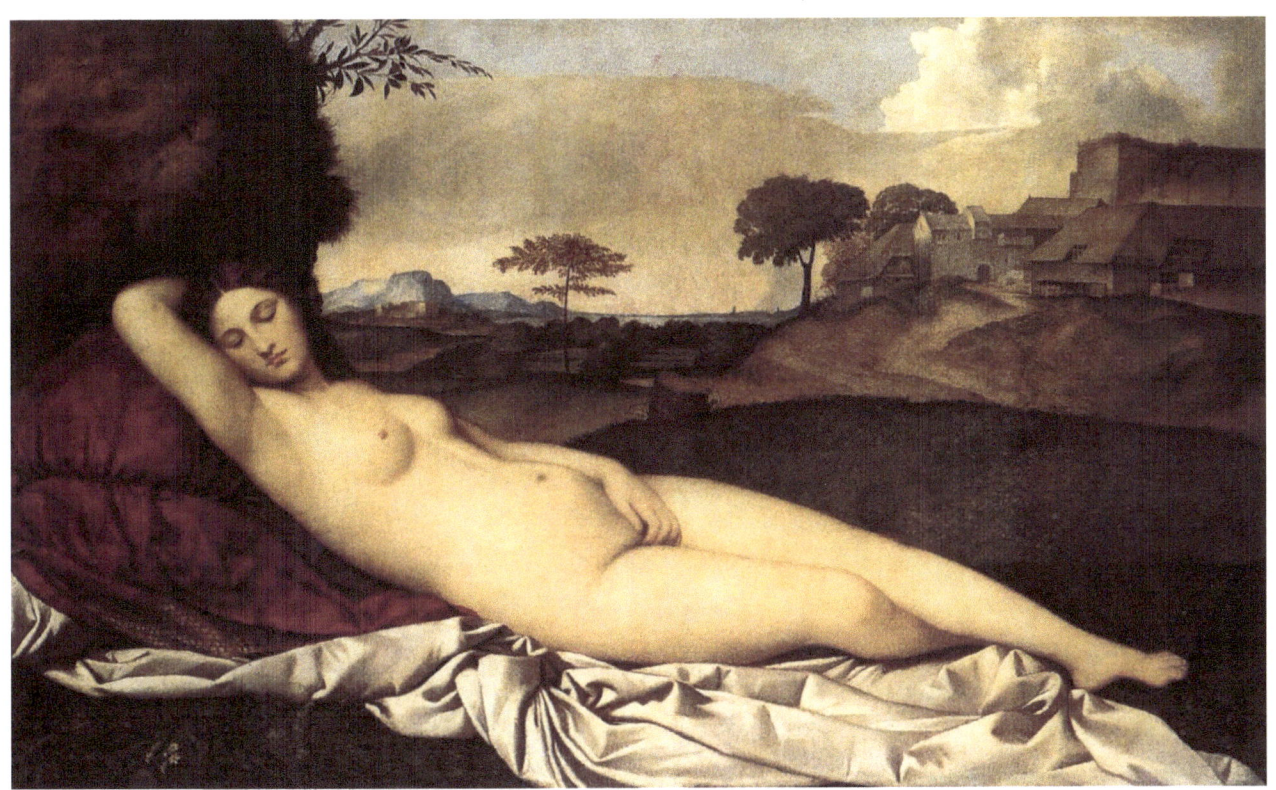

The Sleeping Venus--Giorgione—1510--High Renaissance

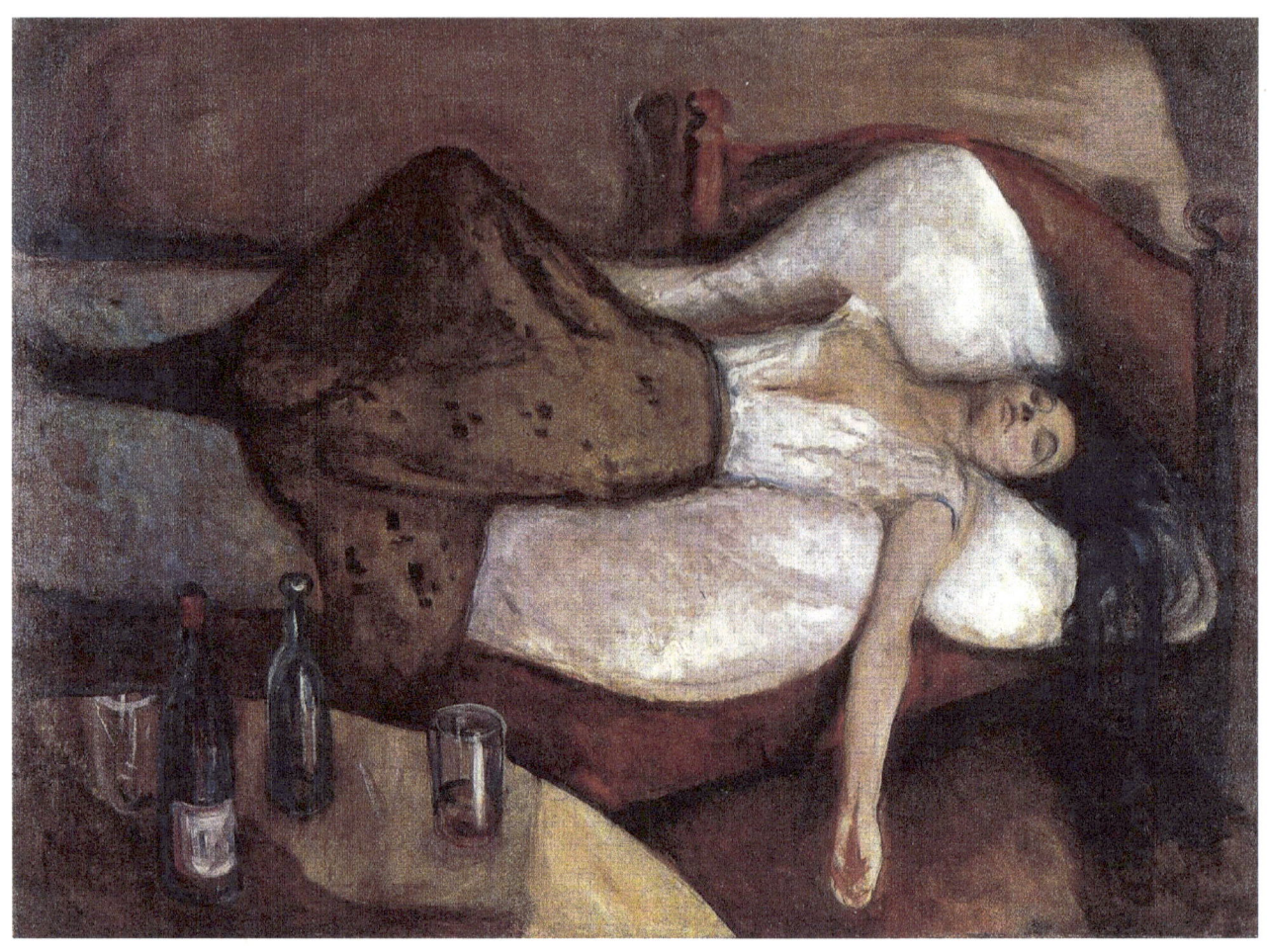

The Day After --Edvard Munch—1895--Expressionism

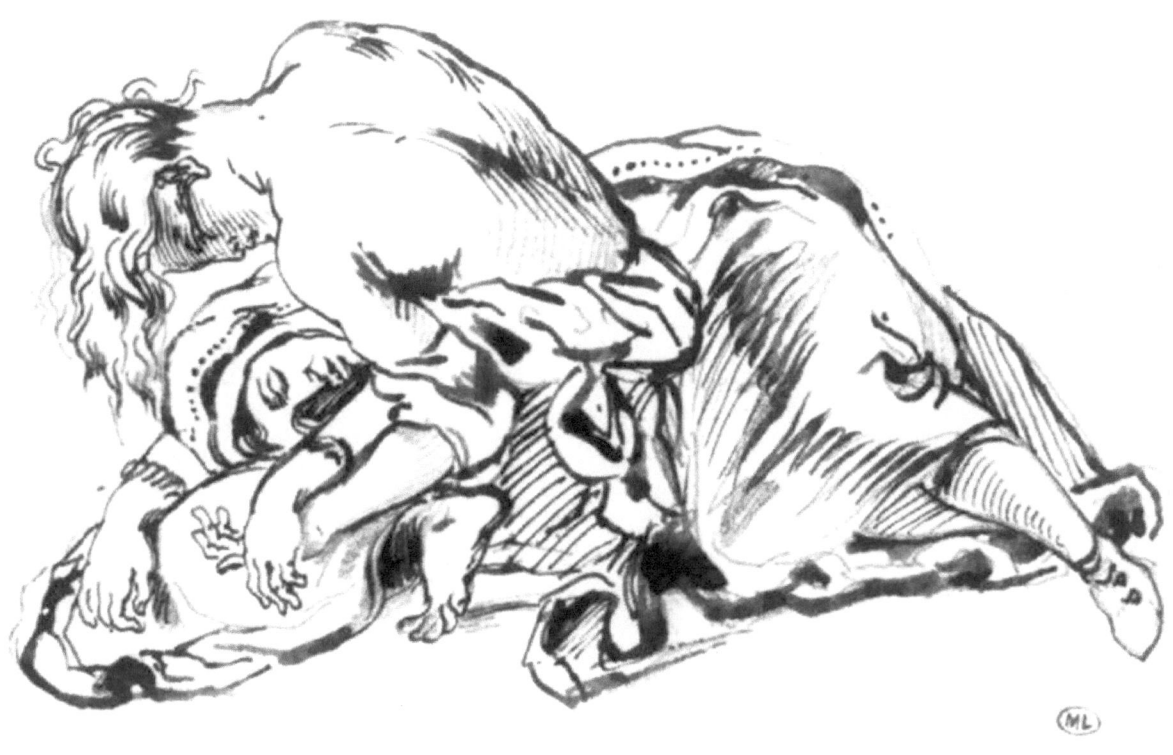

Yound Woman Leaning over a Woman Stretched out on the Ground

Eugene Delacroix—1840--Romanticism

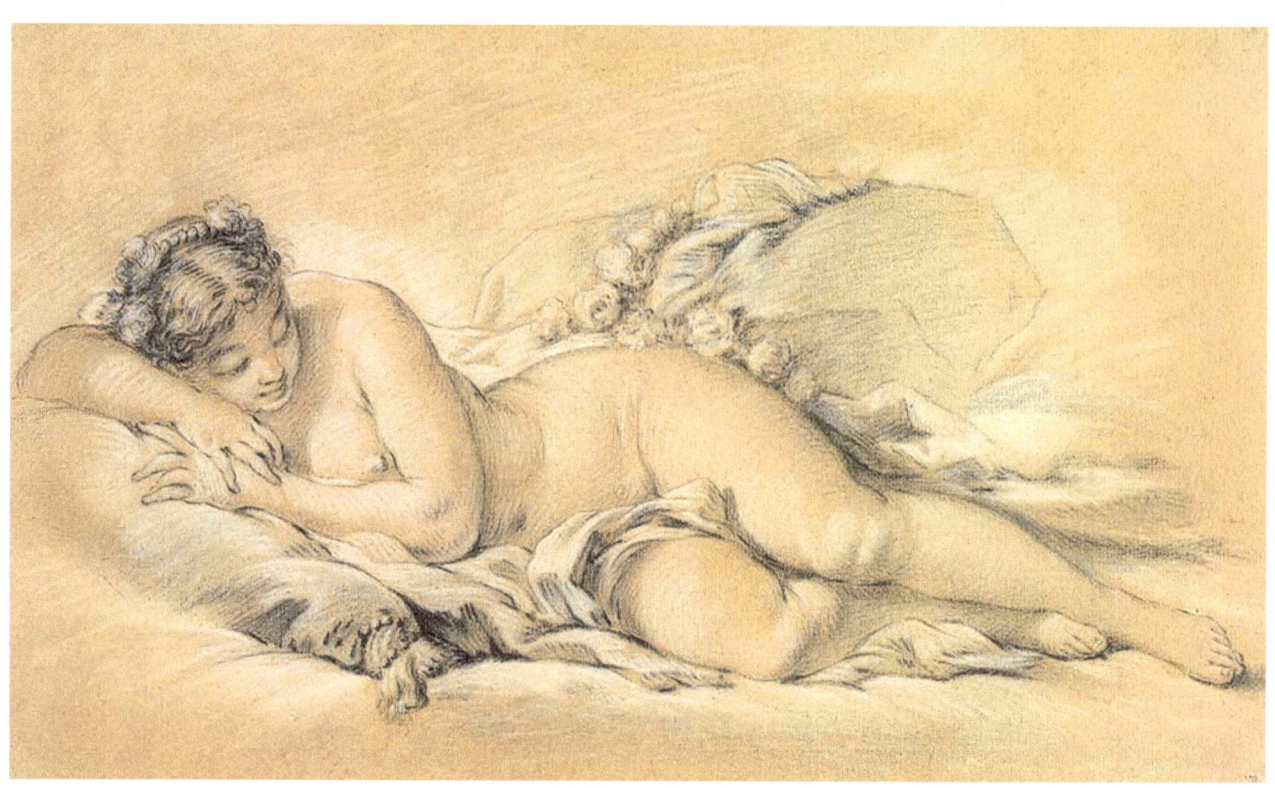

Young Woman Sleeping--Francois Boucher—1760--Rococo

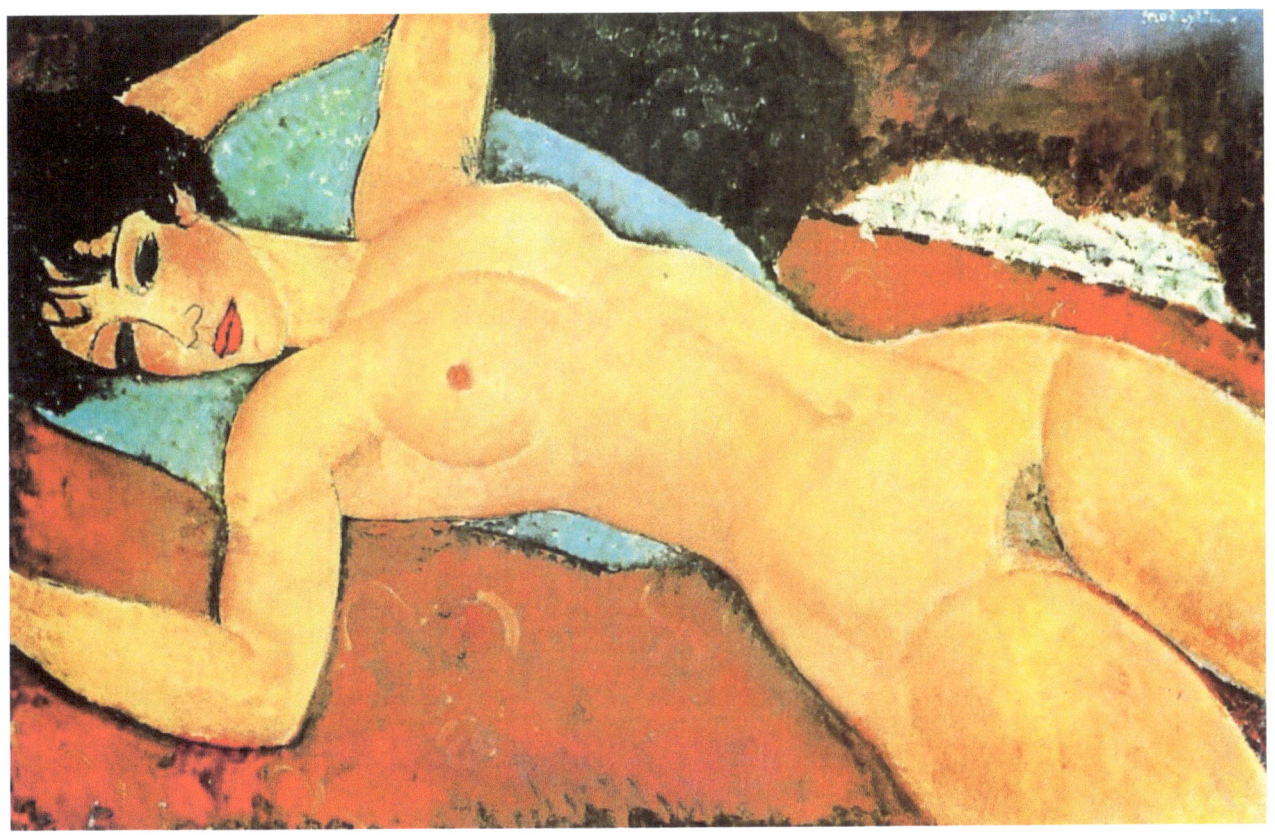

Sleeping Nude with Arms Open (Red Nude)--Amedeo Modigliani--1917

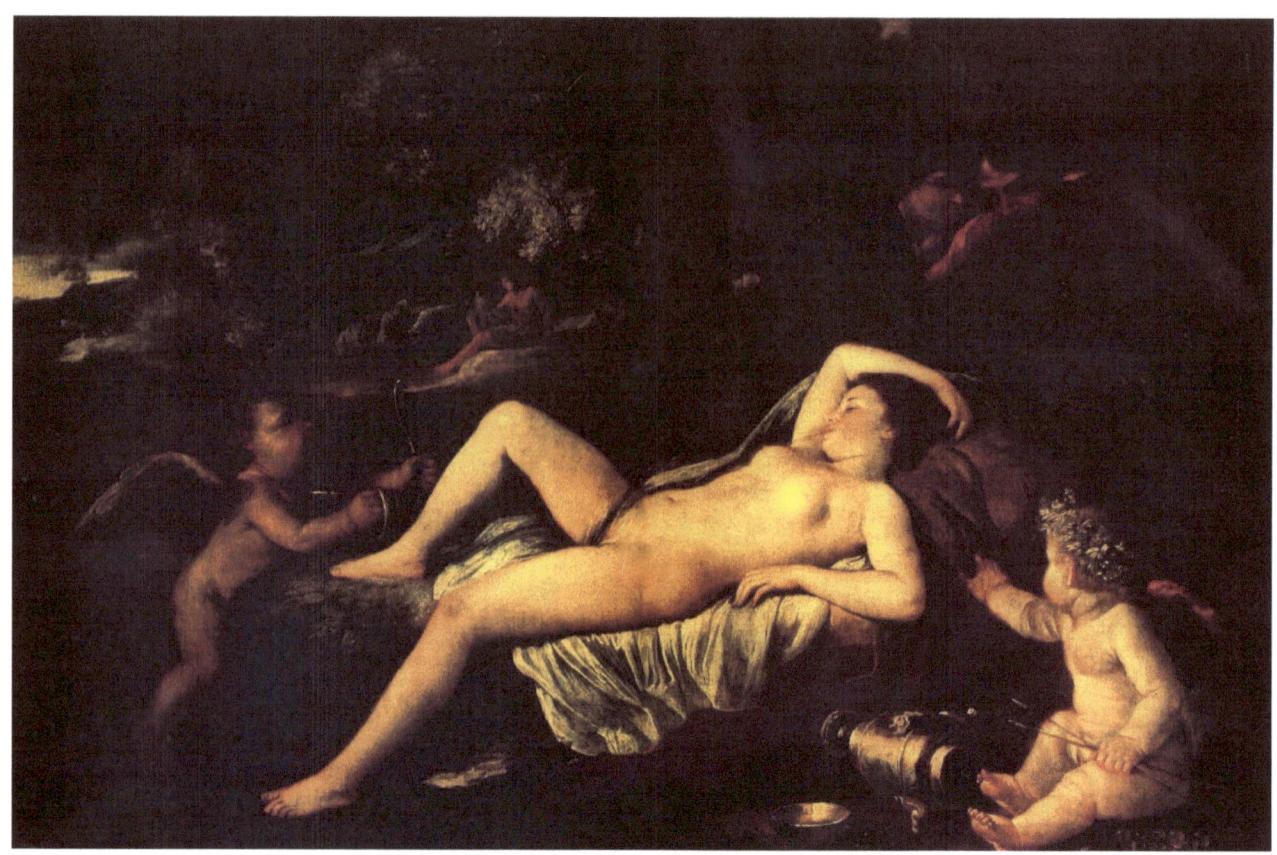

Sleeping Venus and Cupid--Nicolas Poussin—1630--Classicism

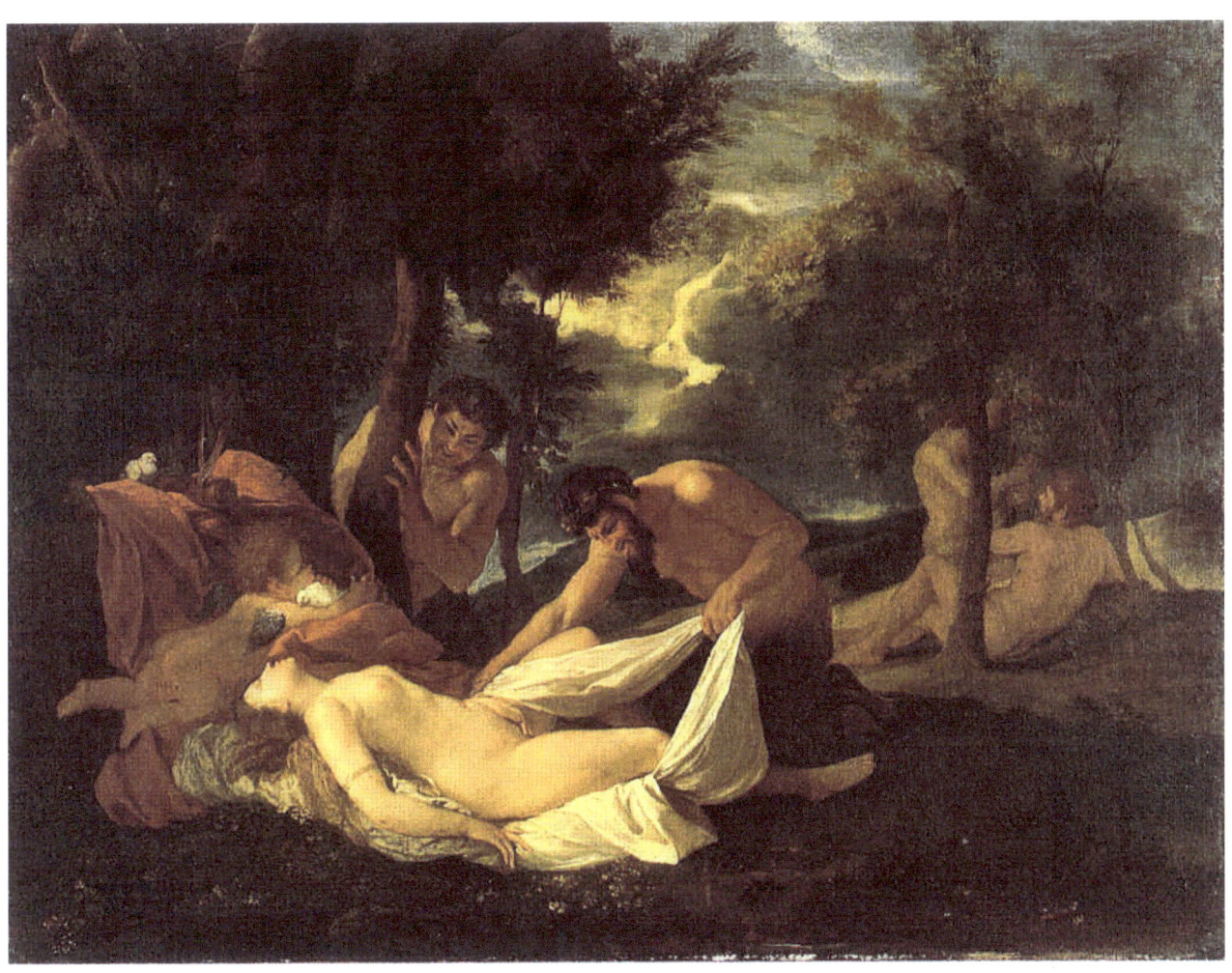

Sleeping Venus and Cupid--Nicolas Poussin—1630--Classicism

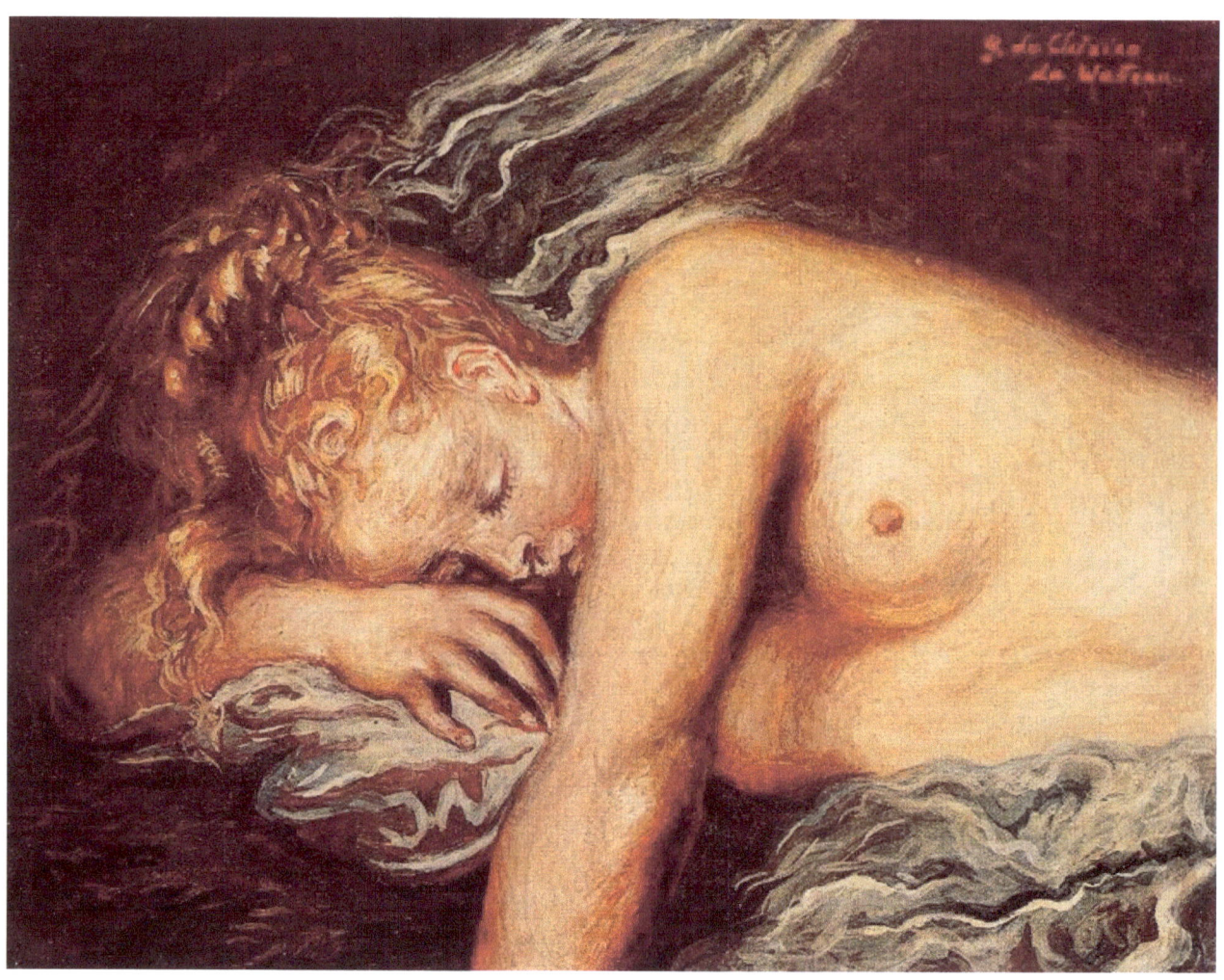

Girl Asleep--Giorgio de Chirico--Neo-baroque

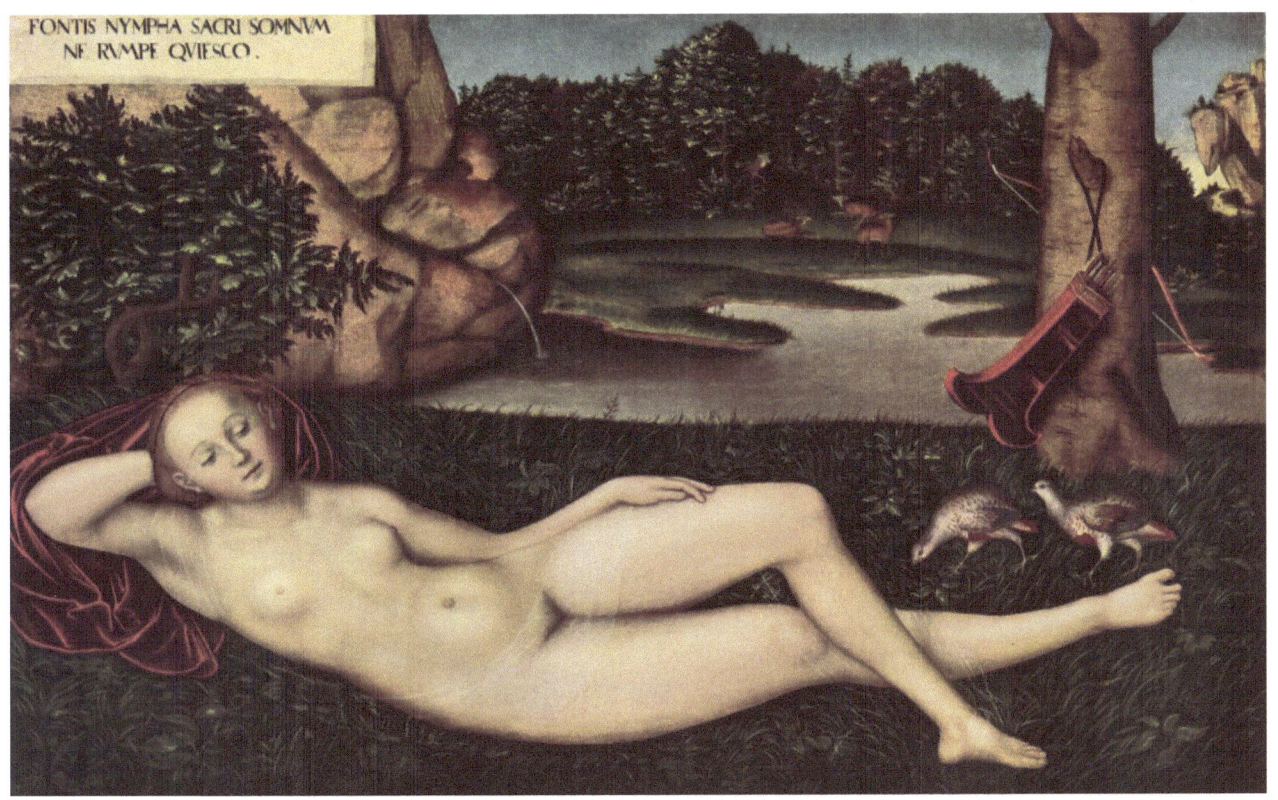

Sleeping Nymph of the Spring --Lucas Cranach the Elder --Northern Renaissance

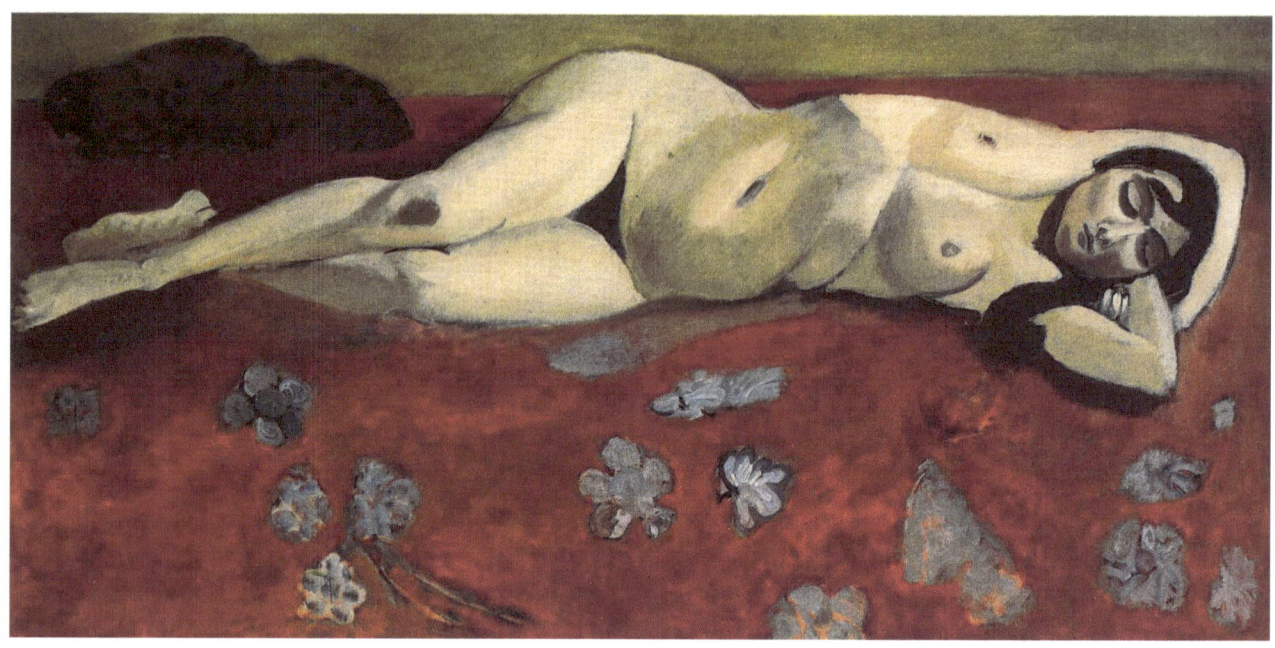

Sleeping Nude on a Red Background--Henri Matisse—1916--Expressionism

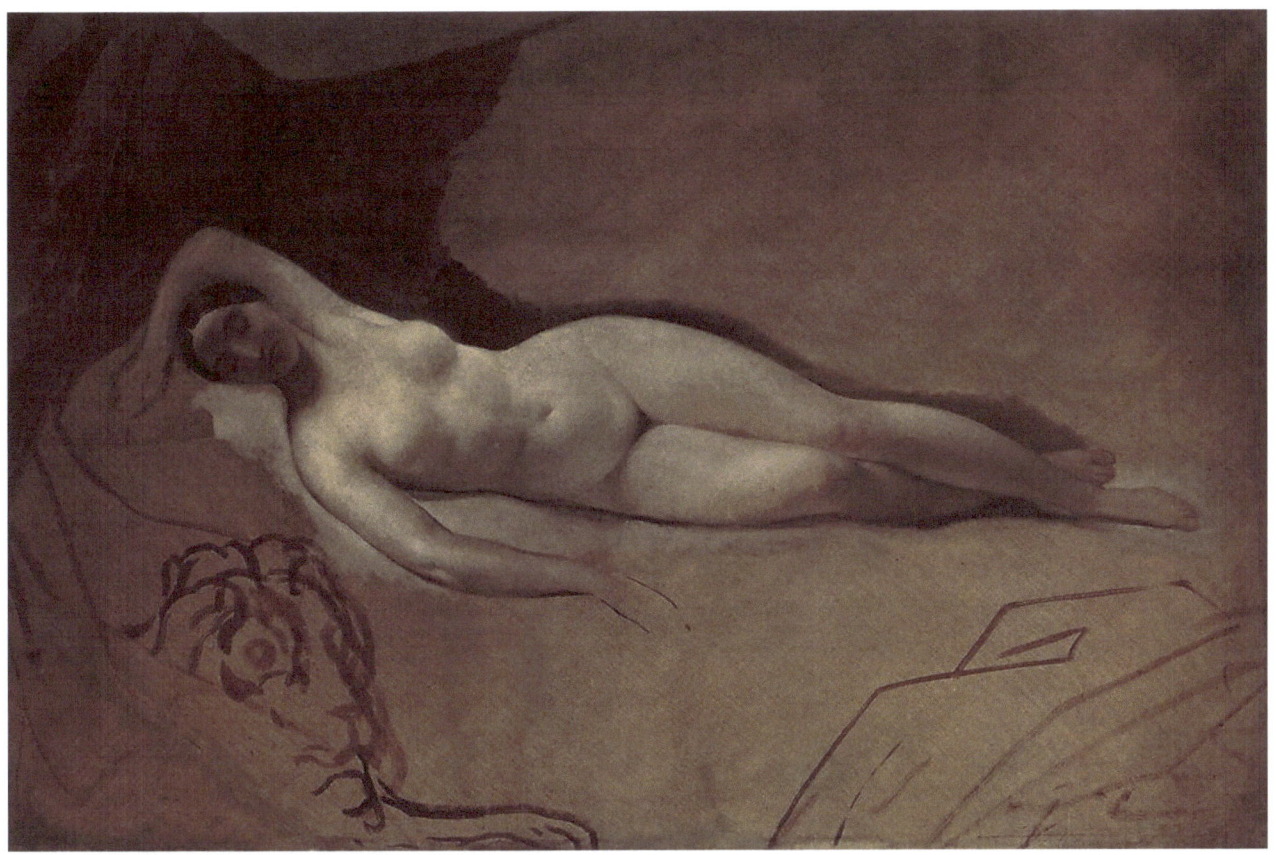

Sleeping Juno--Karl Bryullov--Neoclassicism

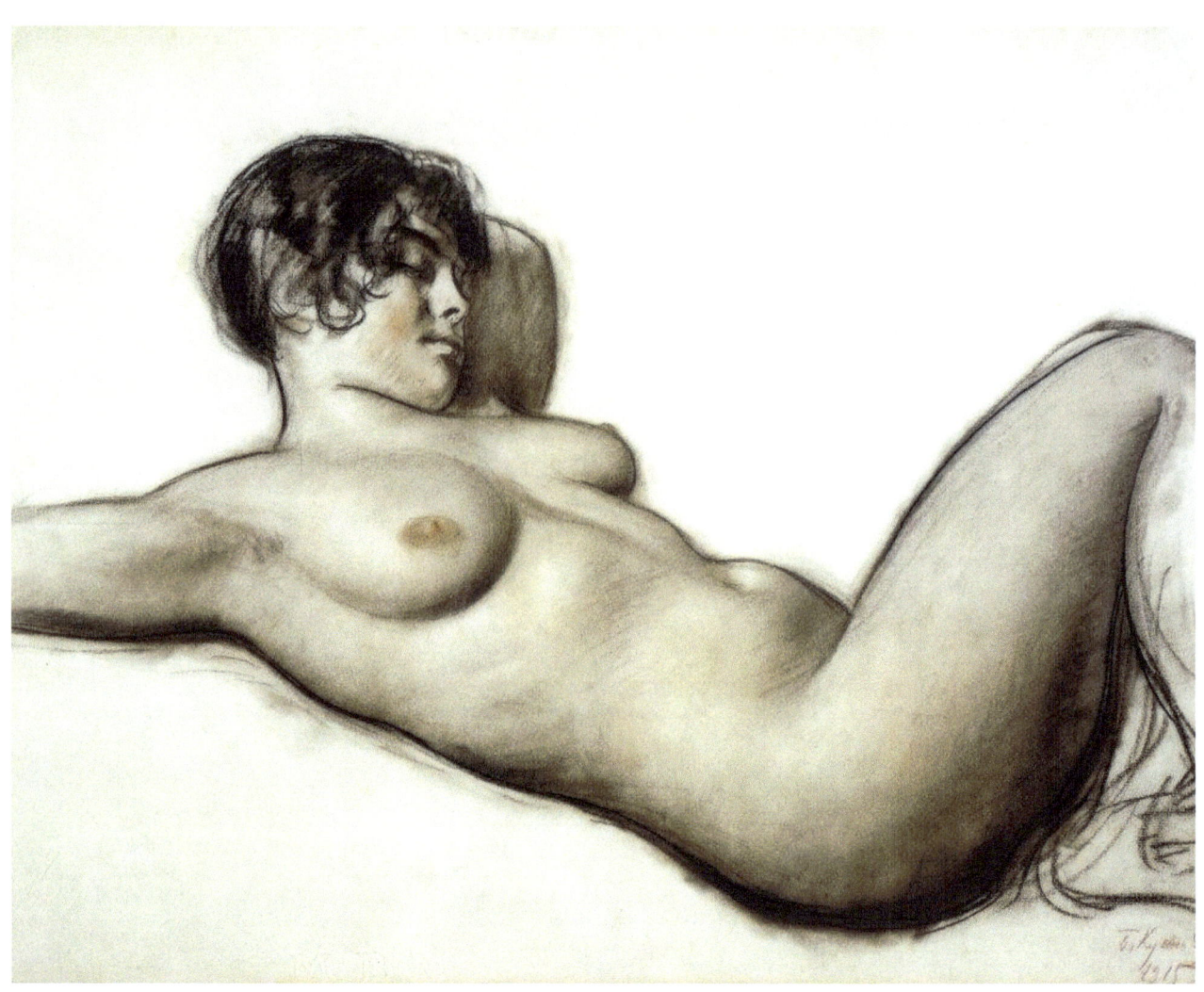

Lying Nude--Boris Kustodiev—1915--Realism

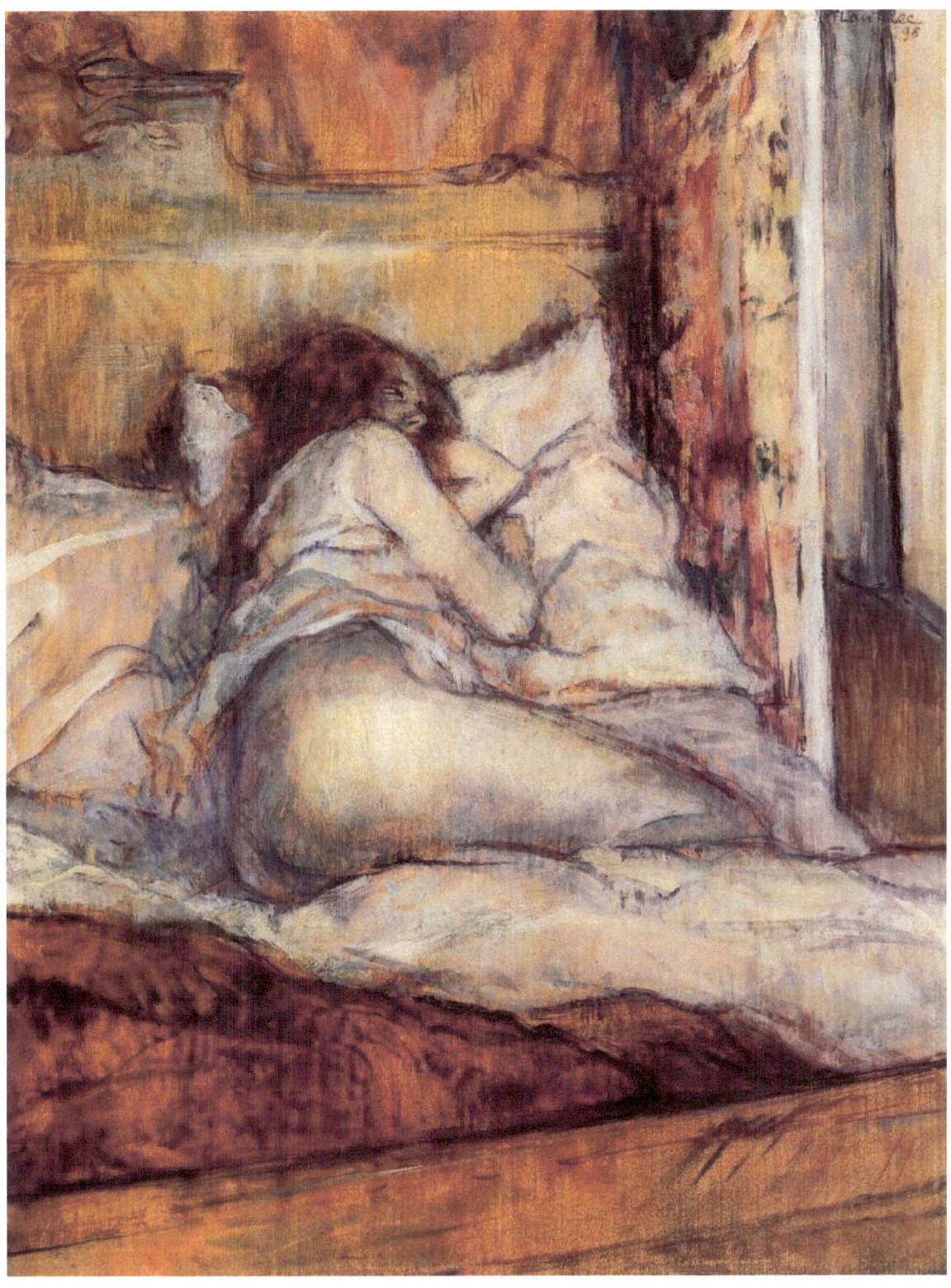

The Bed--Henri de Toulouse-Lautrec—1898--Post-Impressionism

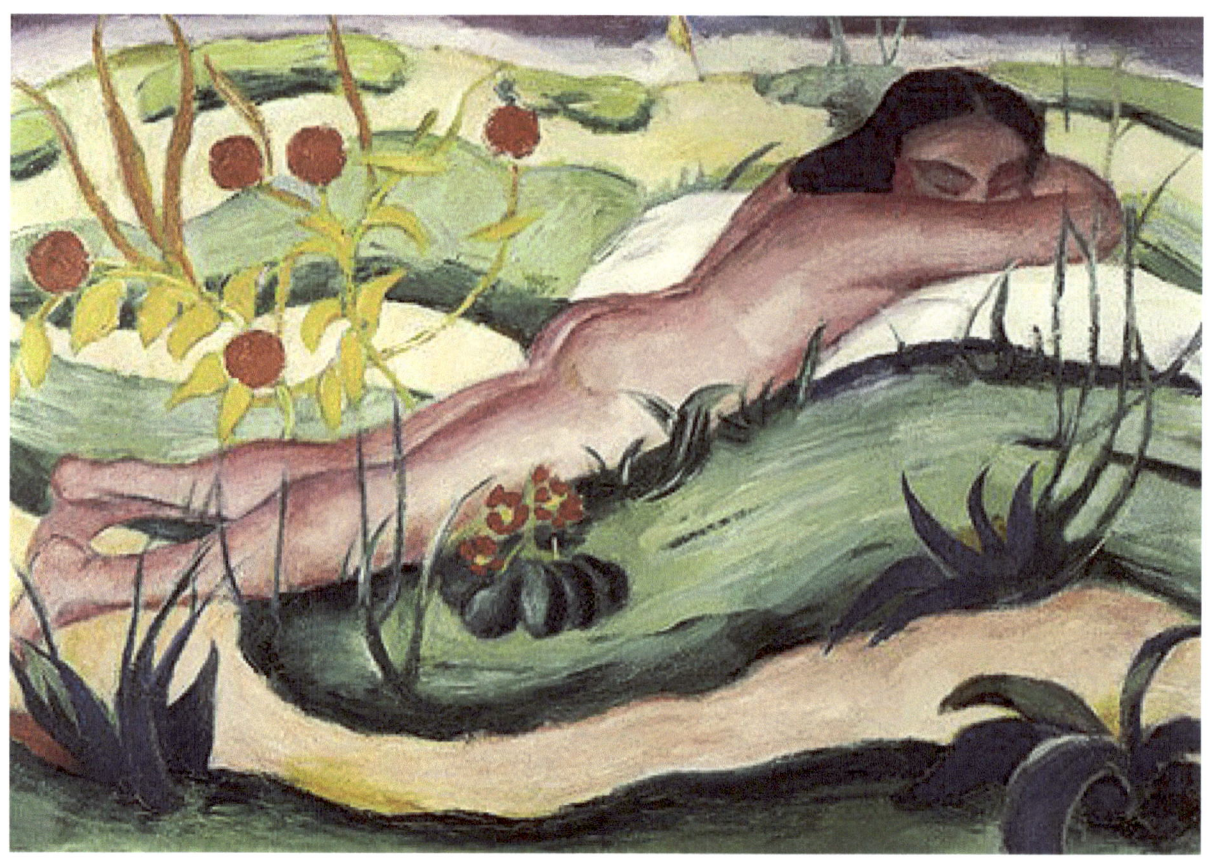

Nude Lying In The Flowers--Franz Marc—1910-- Expressionism

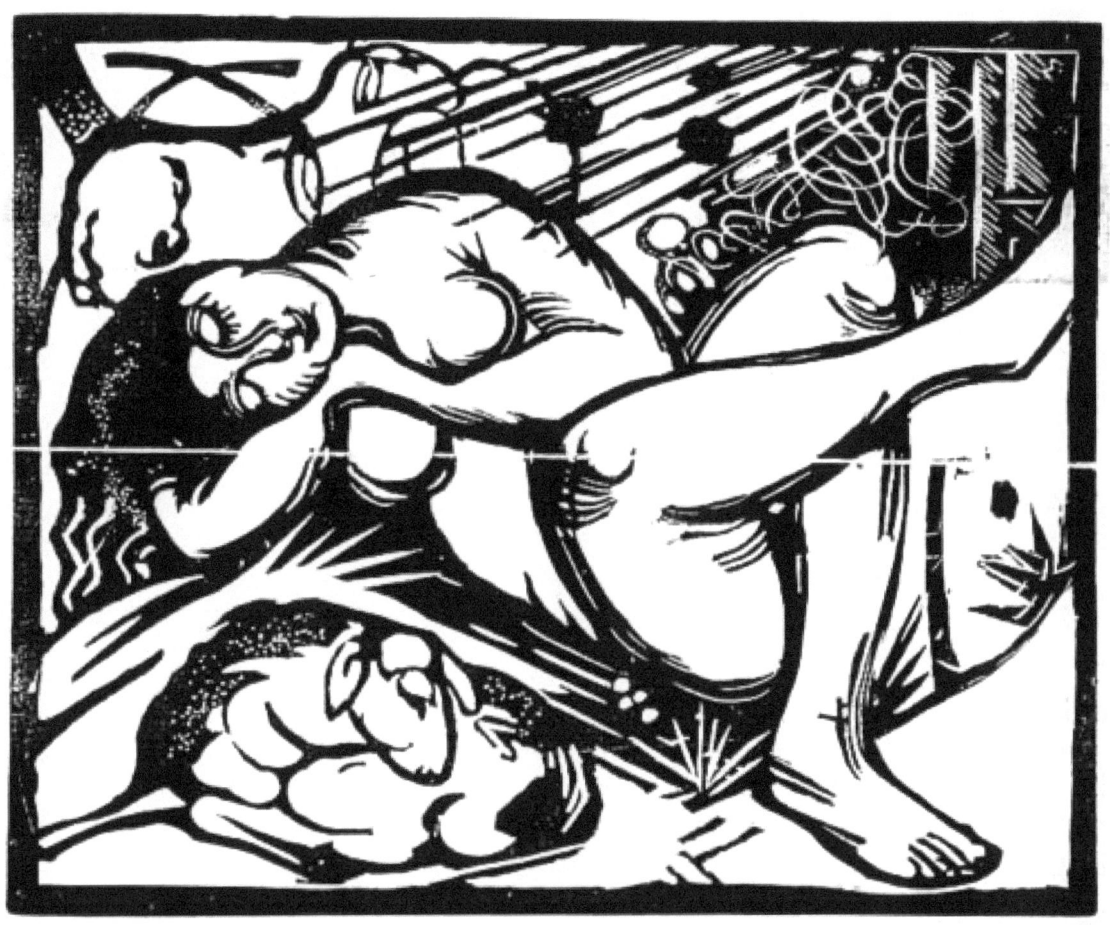

Sleeping Shepherdness--Franz Marc—1912--Expressionism

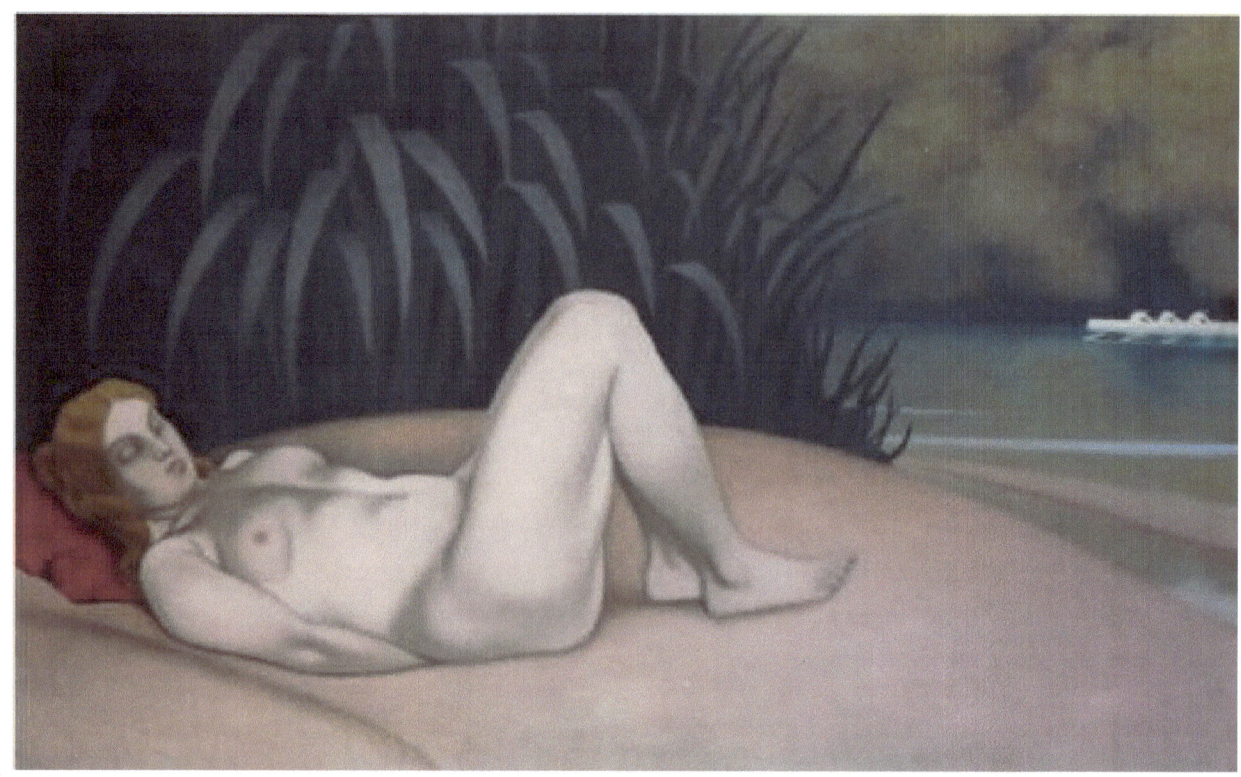

Naked woman sleeping at the edge of the water--Felix Vallotton—1921--Magic Realism

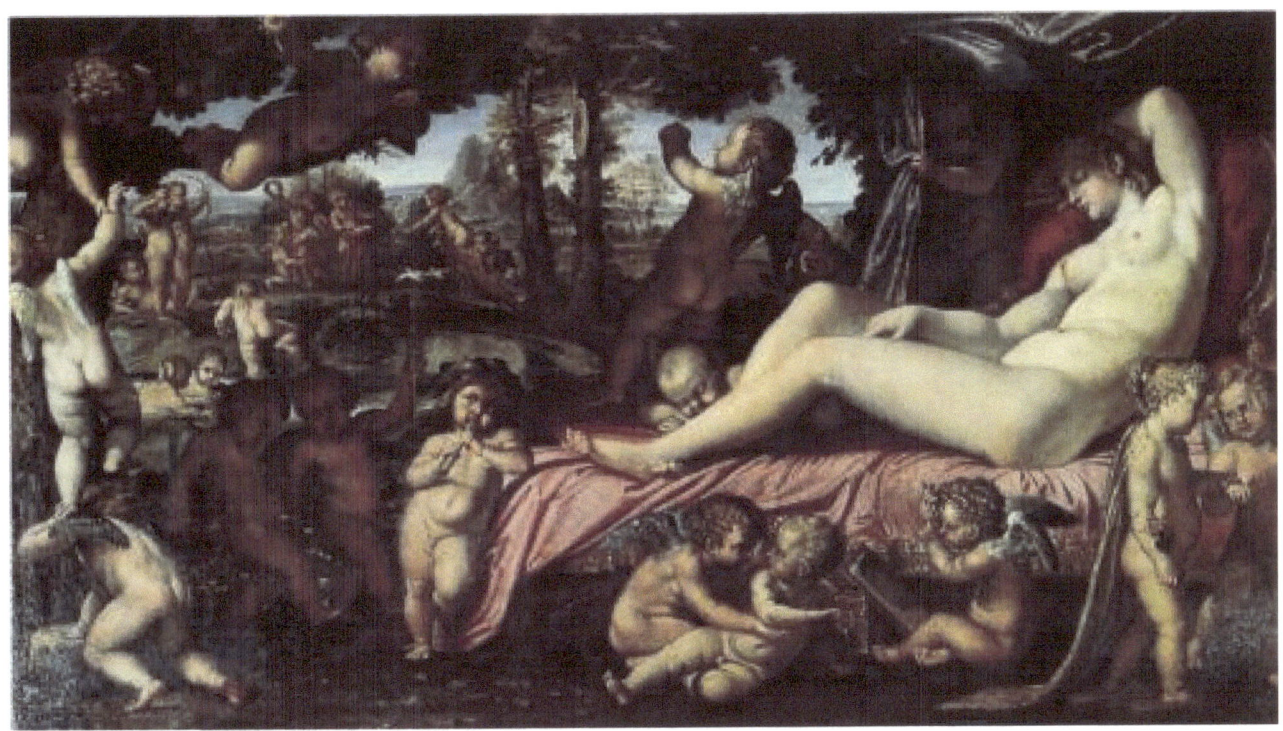

Sleeping Venus--Annibale Carracci—1602-- Baroque

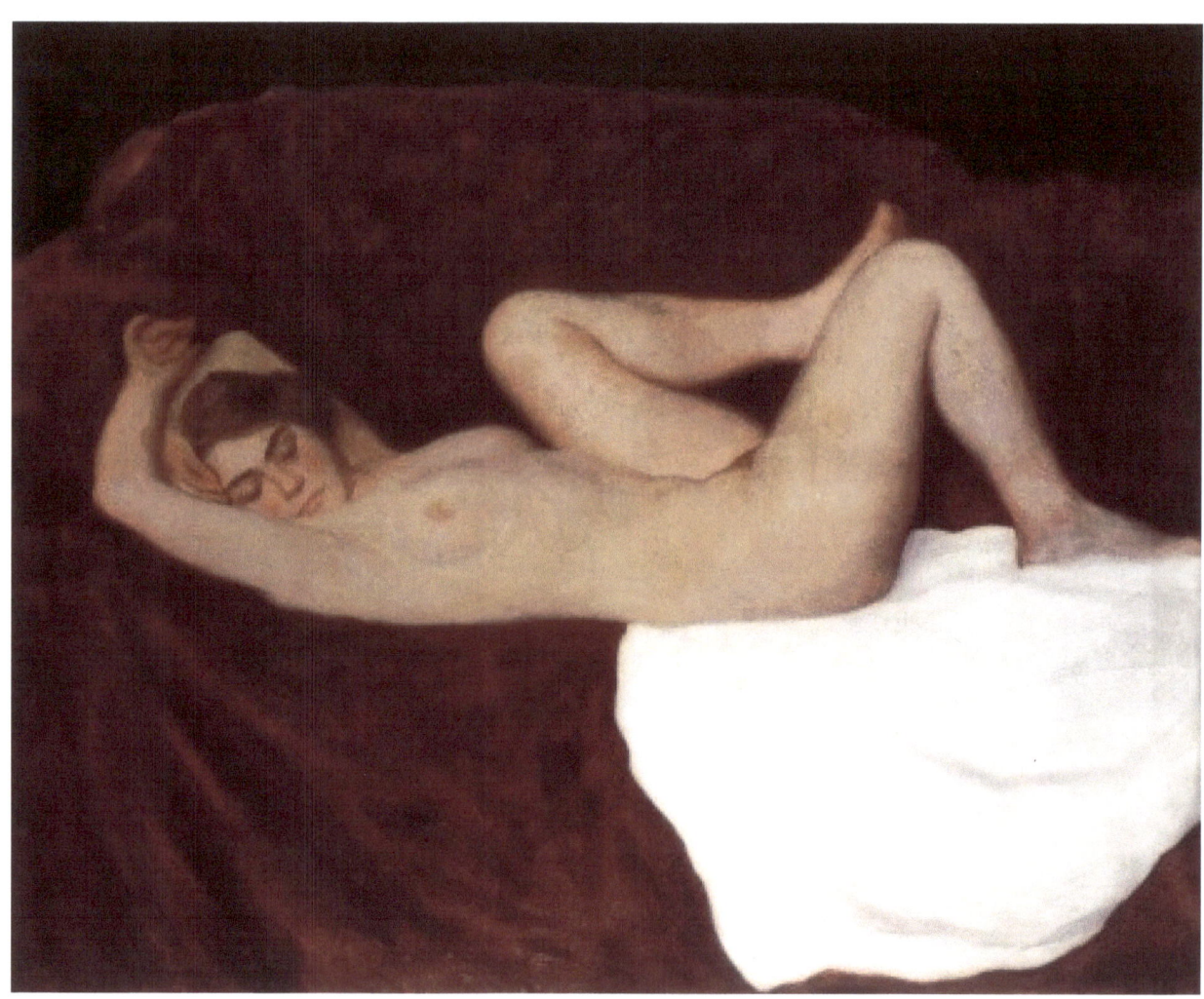

Sleeping Woman--Karoly Ferenczy—1912--Impressionism

www.ingramcontent.com/pod-product-compliance
Lightning Source LLC
Chambersburg PA
CBHW050357180526
45159CB00005B/2051